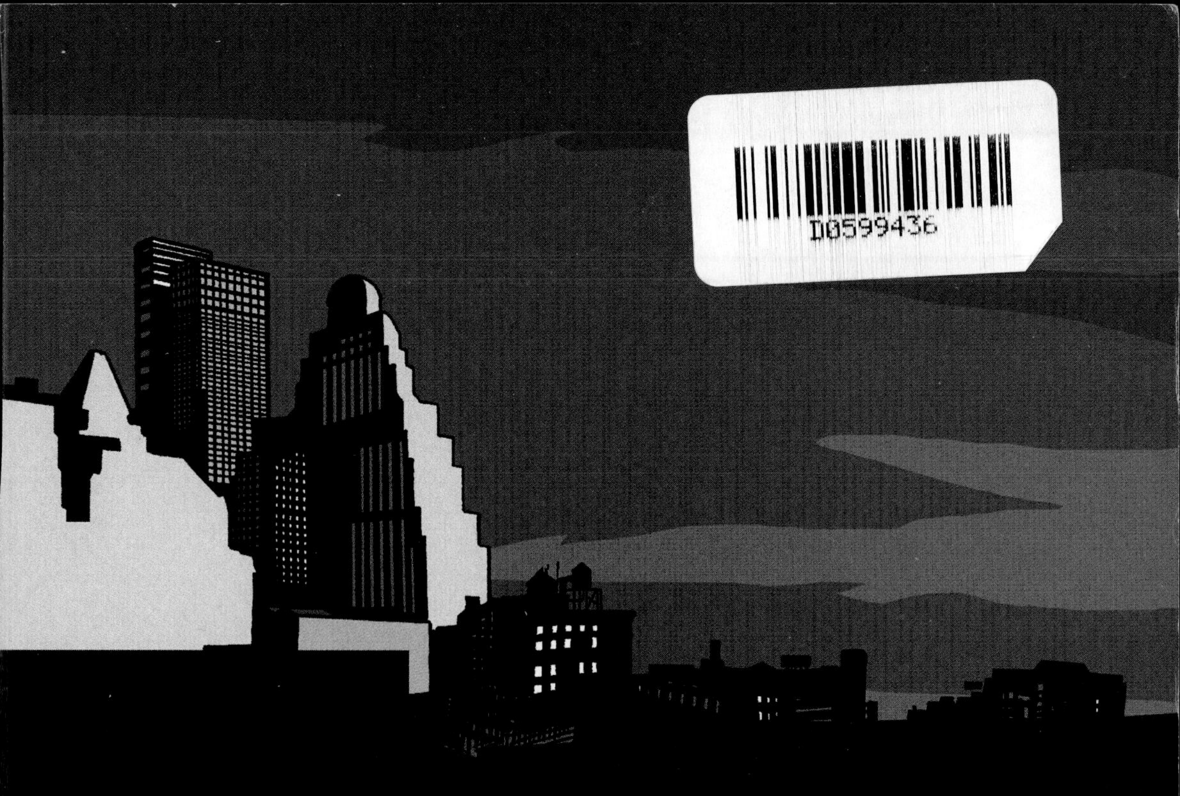

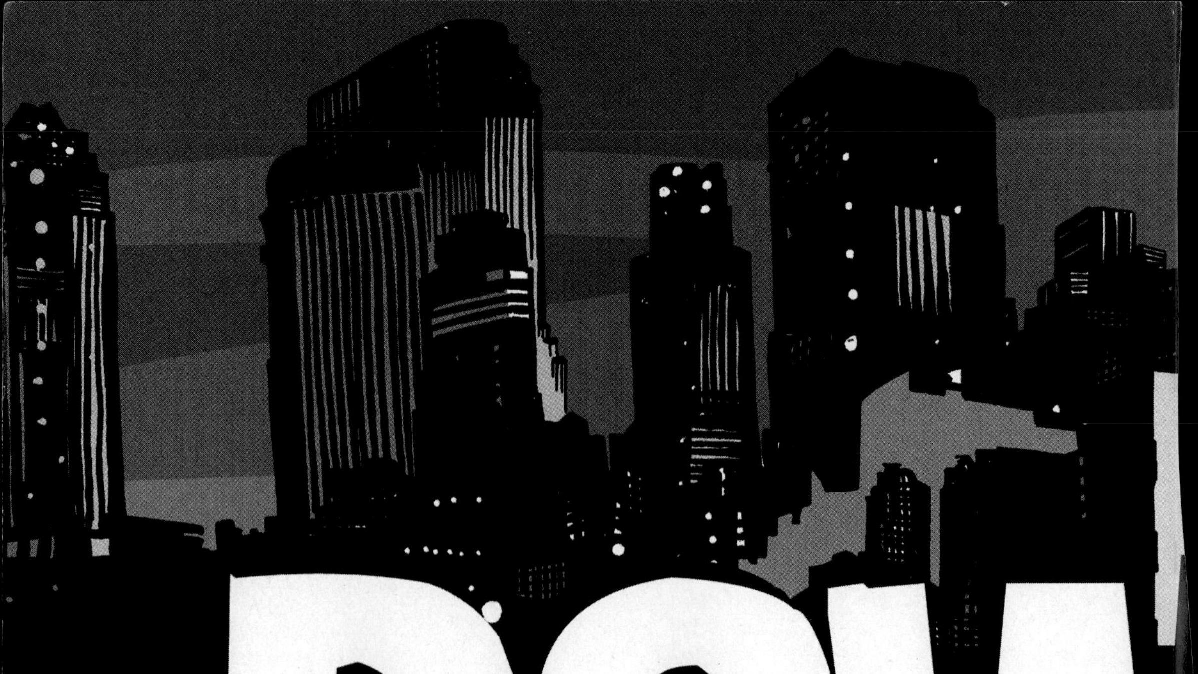

POW

CREATED AN

BRIAN MICHAEL BEND

COLOR ART BY

PAT GARRAHY

SEPARATION ASSISTS BY OJO CALIENTE STUDIOS

LETTERING BY

GARRAHY AND BEND

ERS

PRODUCED BY
AND **MIKE AVON OEMING**

EDITOR
K C MCCRORY

BUSINESS AFFAIRS
ALISA BENDIS

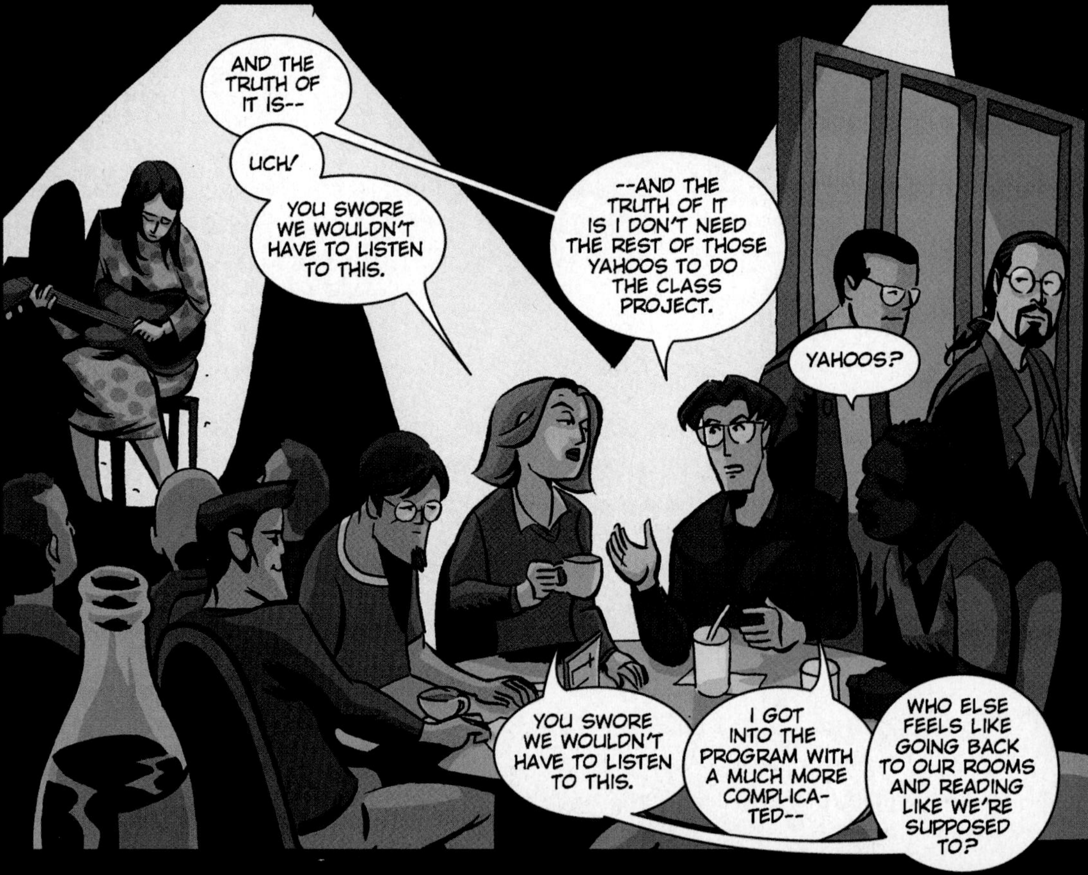
AND THE TRUTH OF IT IS--
UCH!
YOU SWORE WE WOULDN'T HAVE TO LISTEN TO THIS.
--AND THE TRUTH OF IT IS I DON'T NEED THE REST OF THOSE YAHOOS TO DO THE CLASS PROJECT.
YAHOOS?
YOU SWORE WE WOULDN'T HAVE TO LISTEN TO THIS.
I GOT INTO THE PROGRAM WITH A MUCH MORE COMPLICA-TED--
WHO ELSE FEELS LIKE GOING BACK TO OUR ROOMS AND READING LIKE WE'RE SUPPOSED TO?

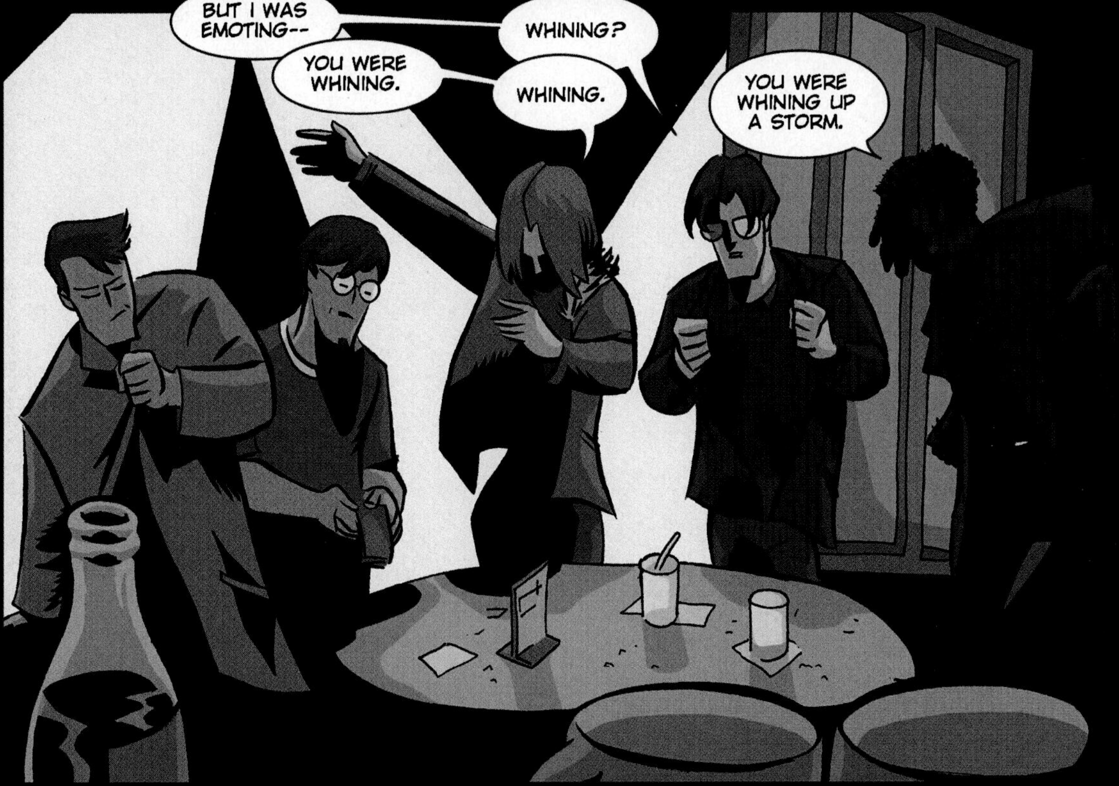
BUT I WAS EMOTING--
WHINING?
YOU WERE WHINING.
WHINING.
YOU WERE WHINING UP A STORM.

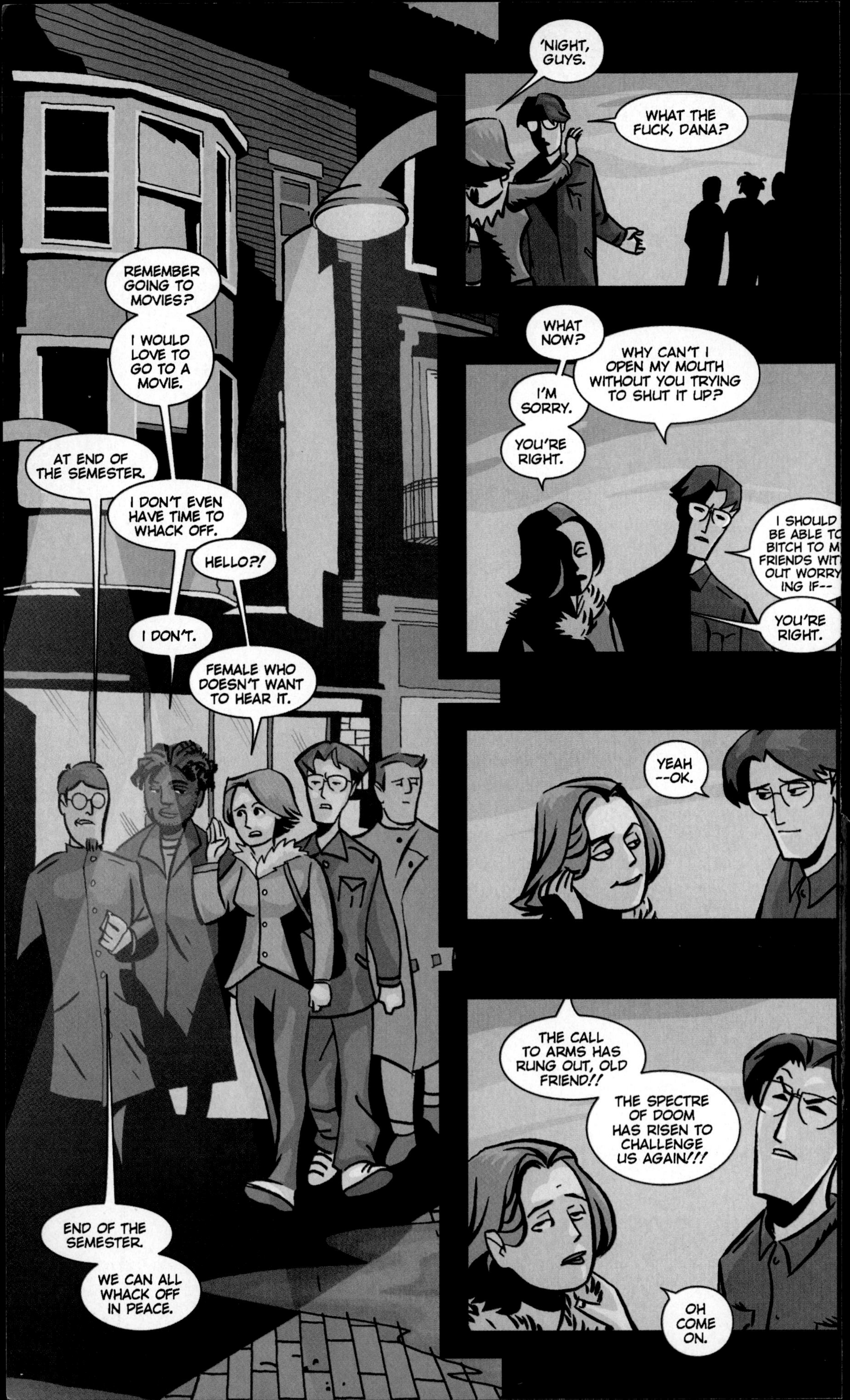
REMEMBER GOING TO MOVIES?
I WOULD LOVE TO GO TO A MOVIE.
AT END OF THE SEMESTER.
I DON'T EVEN HAVE TIME TO WHACK OFF.
HELLO?!
I DON'T.
FEMALE WHO DOESN'T WANT TO HEAR IT.
END OF THE SEMESTER.
WE CAN ALL WHACK OFF IN PEACE.
'NIGHT, GUYS.
WHAT THE FUCK, DANA?
WHAT NOW?
WHY CAN'T I OPEN MY MOUTH WITHOUT YOU TRYING TO SHUT IT UP?
I'M SORRY.
YOU'RE RIGHT.
I SHOULD BE ABLE TO BITCH TO MY FRIENDS WITH-OUT WORRY-ING IF--
YOU'RE RIGHT.
YEAH --OK.
THE CALL TO ARMS HAS RUNG OUT, OLD FRIEND!!
THE SPECTRE OF DOOM HAS RISEN TO CHALLENGE US AGAIN!!!
OH COME ON.

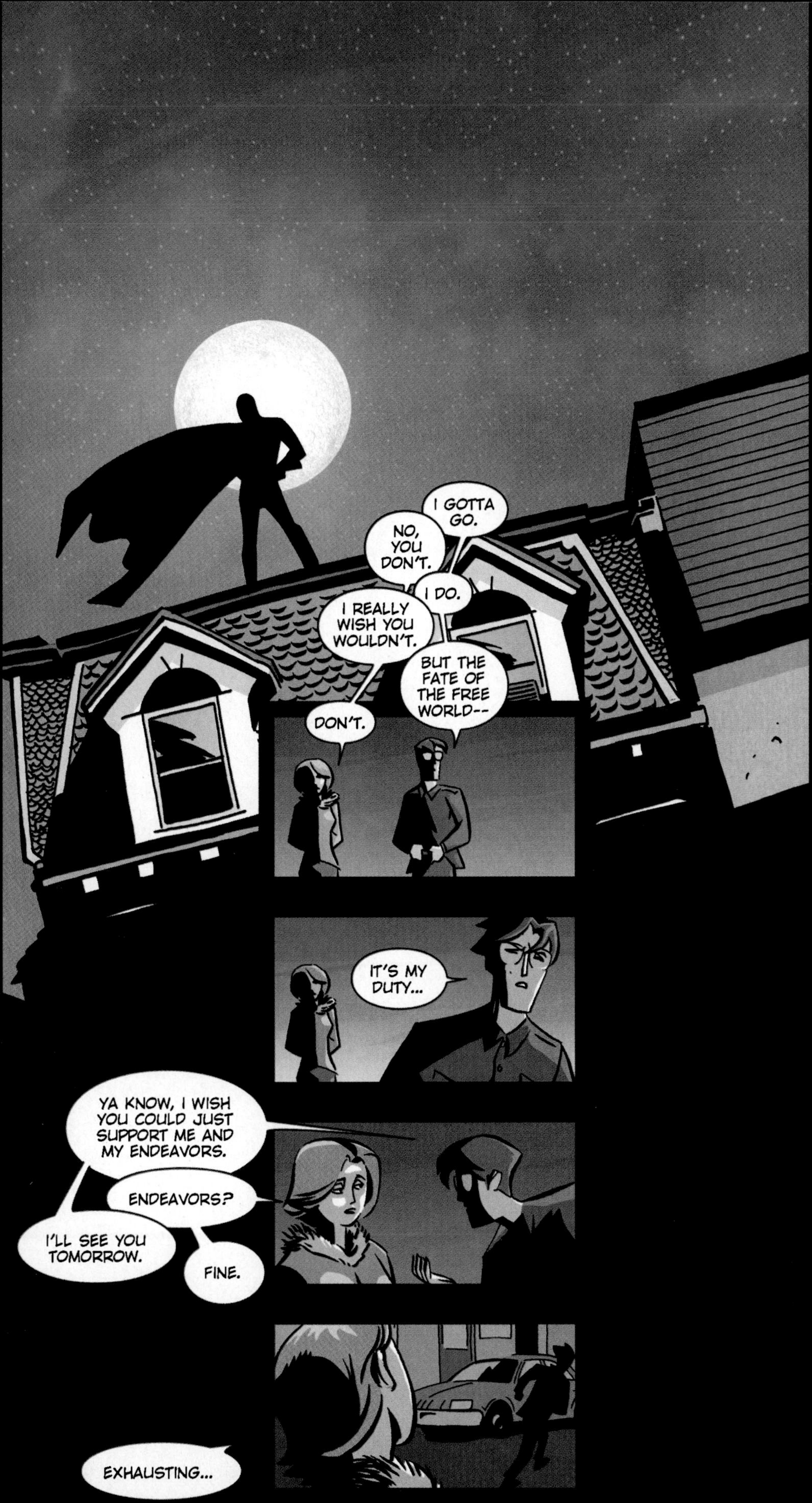
I GOTTA GO.
NO, YOU DON'T.
I DO.
I REALLY WISH YOU WOULDN'T.
BUT THE FATE OF THE FREE WORLD--
DON'T.
IT'S MY DUTY...
YA KNOW, I WISH YOU COULD JUST SUPPORT ME AND MY ENDEAVORS.
ENDEAVORS?
I'LL SEE YOU TOMORROW.
FINE.
EXHAUSTING...

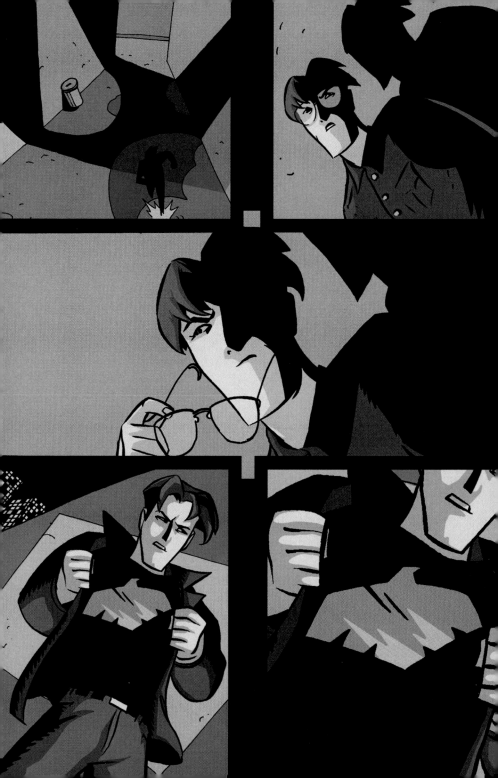

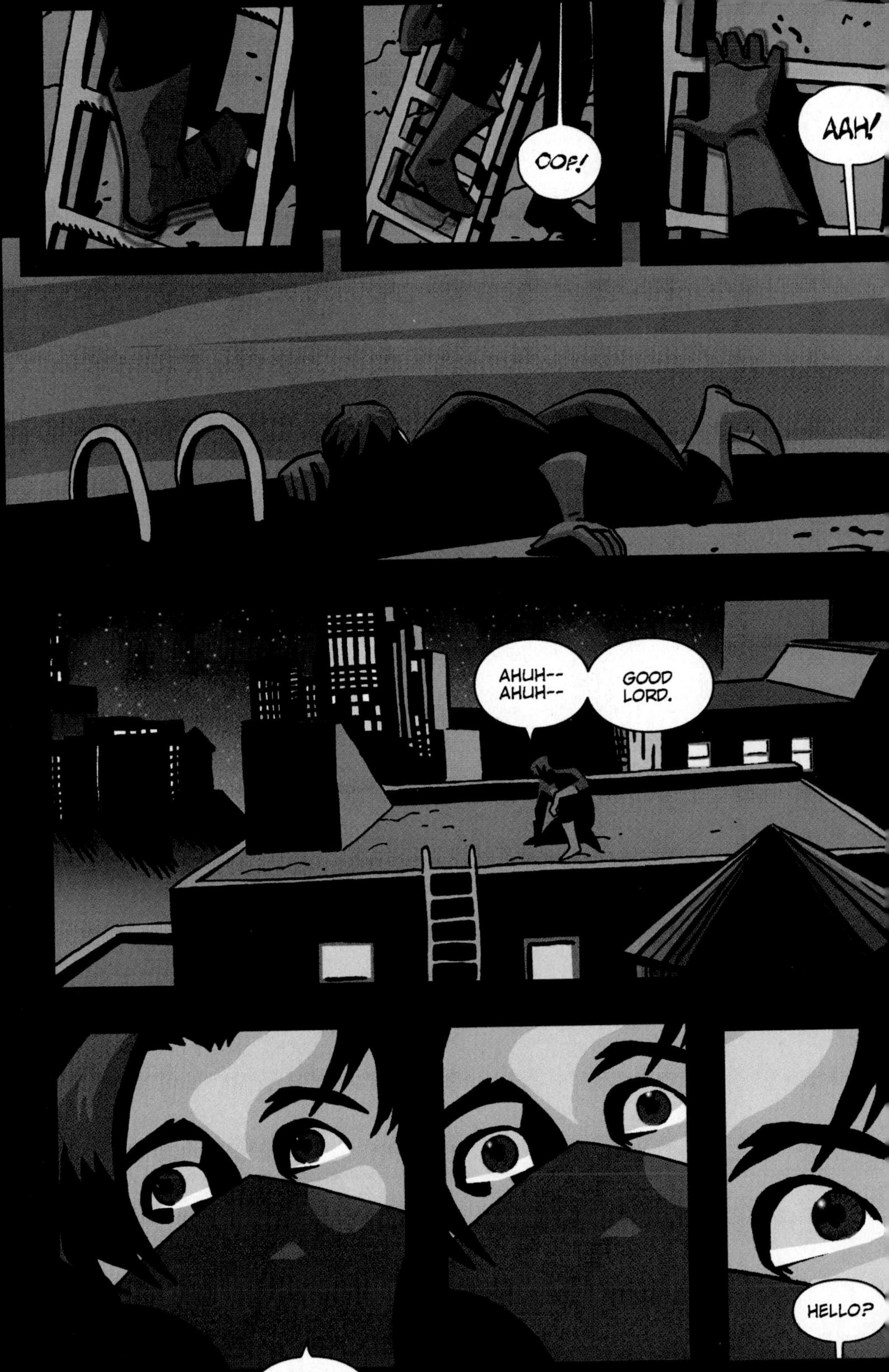
OOF!
AAH!
AHUH--
AHUH--
GOOD
LORD.
SO--
UH--
HELLO?
HELLO?

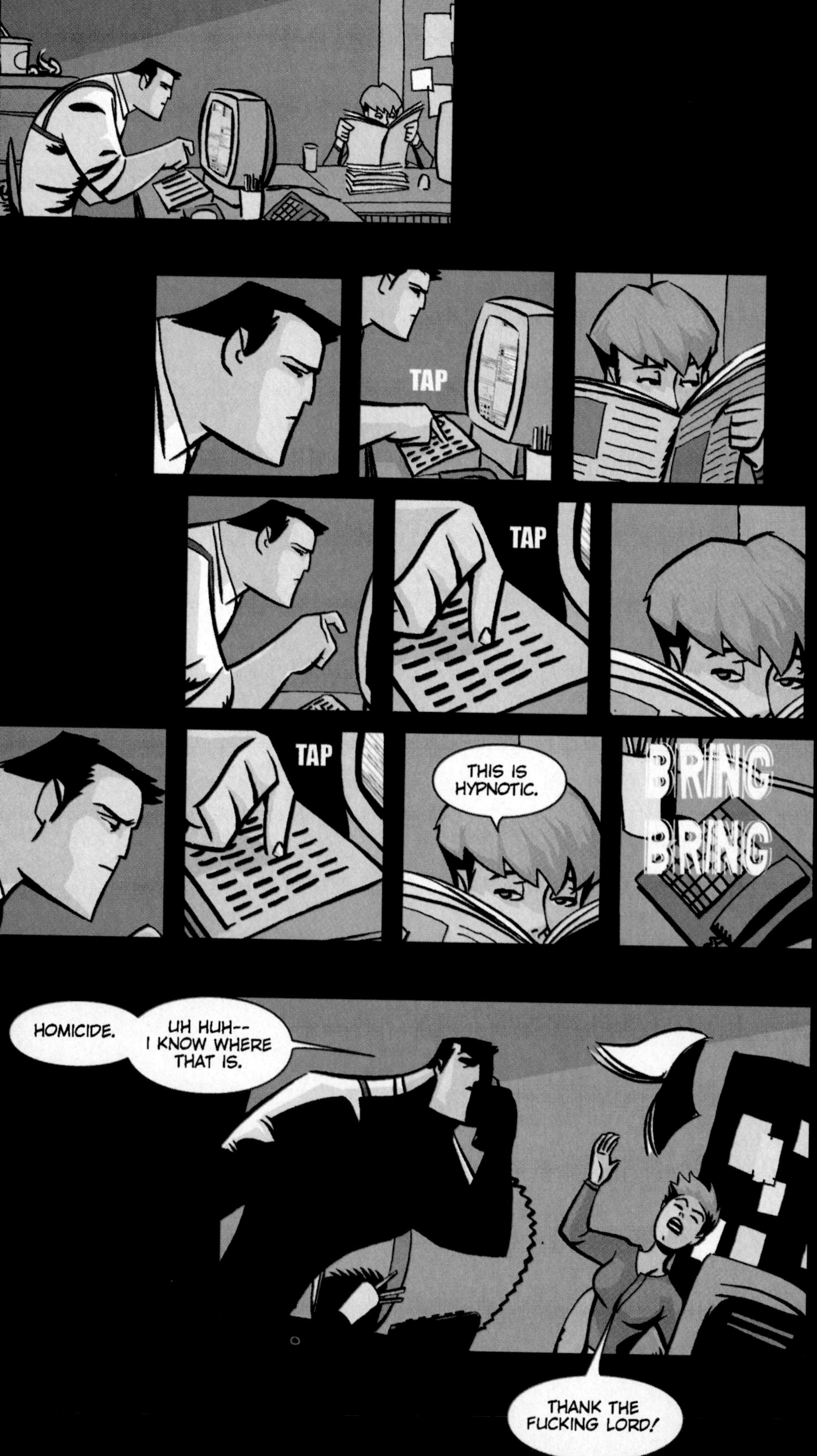
TAP
TAP
TAP
THIS IS HYPNOTIC.
BRING BRING
HOMICIDE.
UH HUH-- I KNOW WHERE THAT IS.
THANK THE FUCKING LORD!

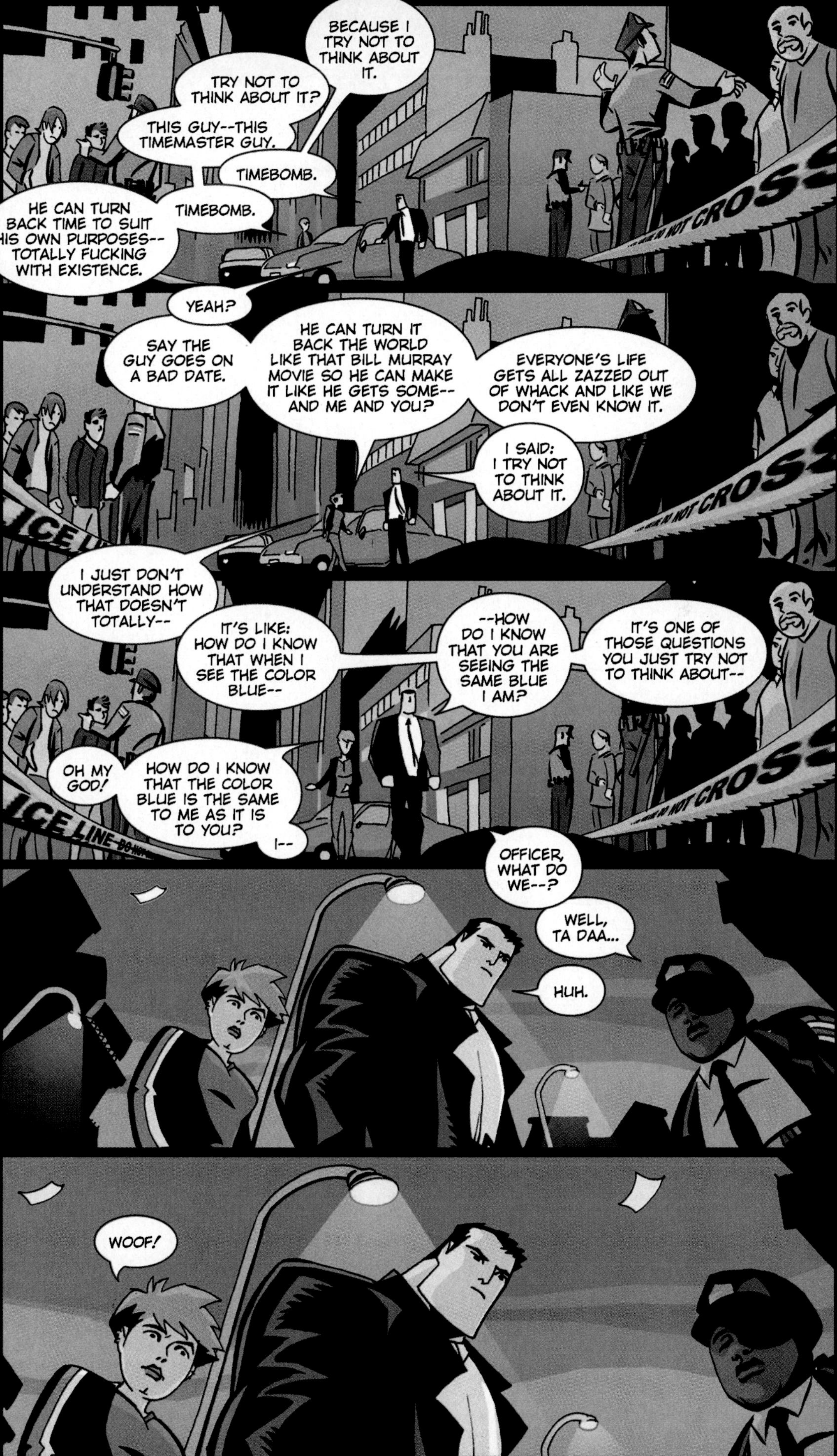
HE CAN TURN BACK TIME TO SUIT HIS OWN PURPOSES-- TOTALLY FUCKING WITH EXISTENCE.
THIS GUY--THIS TIMEMASTER GUY.
TIMEBOMB.
TIMEBOMB.
TRY NOT TO THINK ABOUT IT?
BECAUSE I TRY NOT TO THINK ABOUT IT.
YEAH?
SAY THE GUY GOES ON A BAD DATE.
HE CAN TURN IT BACK THE WORLD LIKE THAT BILL MURRAY MOVIE SO HE CAN MAKE IT LIKE HE GETS SOME-- AND ME AND YOU?
EVERYONE'S LIFE GETS ALL ZAZZED OUT OF WHACK AND LIKE WE DON'T EVEN KNOW IT.
I SAID: I TRY NOT TO THINK ABOUT IT.
DO NOT CROSS
I JUST DON'T UNDERSTAND HOW THAT DOESN'T TOTALLY--
IT'S LIKE: HOW DO I KNOW THAT WHEN I SEE THE COLOR BLUE--
--HOW DO I KNOW THAT YOU ARE SEEING THE SAME BLUE I AM?
IT'S ONE OF THOSE QUESTIONS YOU JUST TRY NOT TO THINK ABOUT--
OH MY GOD!
HOW DO I KNOW THAT THE COLOR BLUE IS THE SAME TO ME AS IT IS TO YOU?
I--
ICE LINE
OFFICER, WHAT DO WE--?
WELL, TA DAA...
HUH.
WOOF!

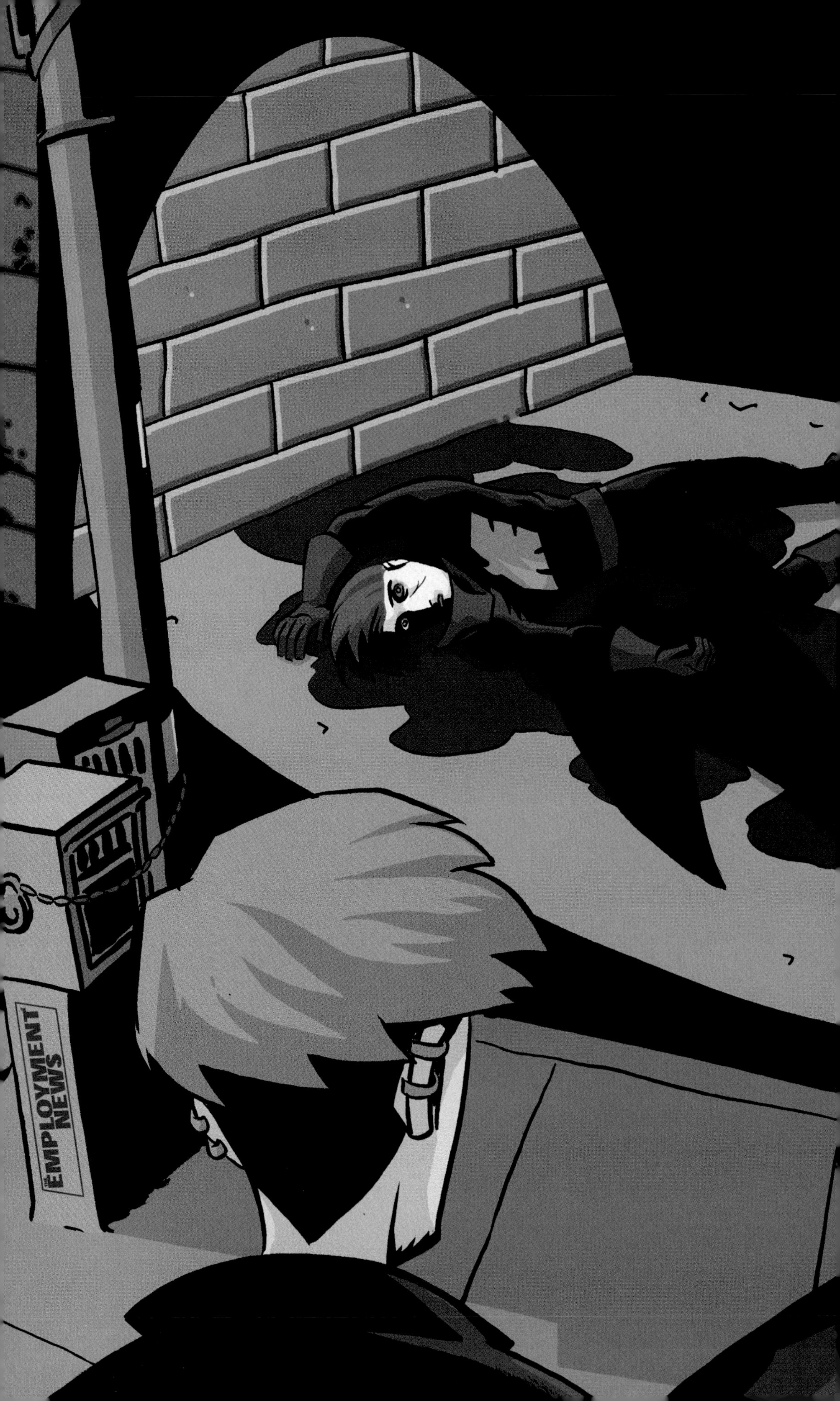
THE EMPLOYMENT NEWS

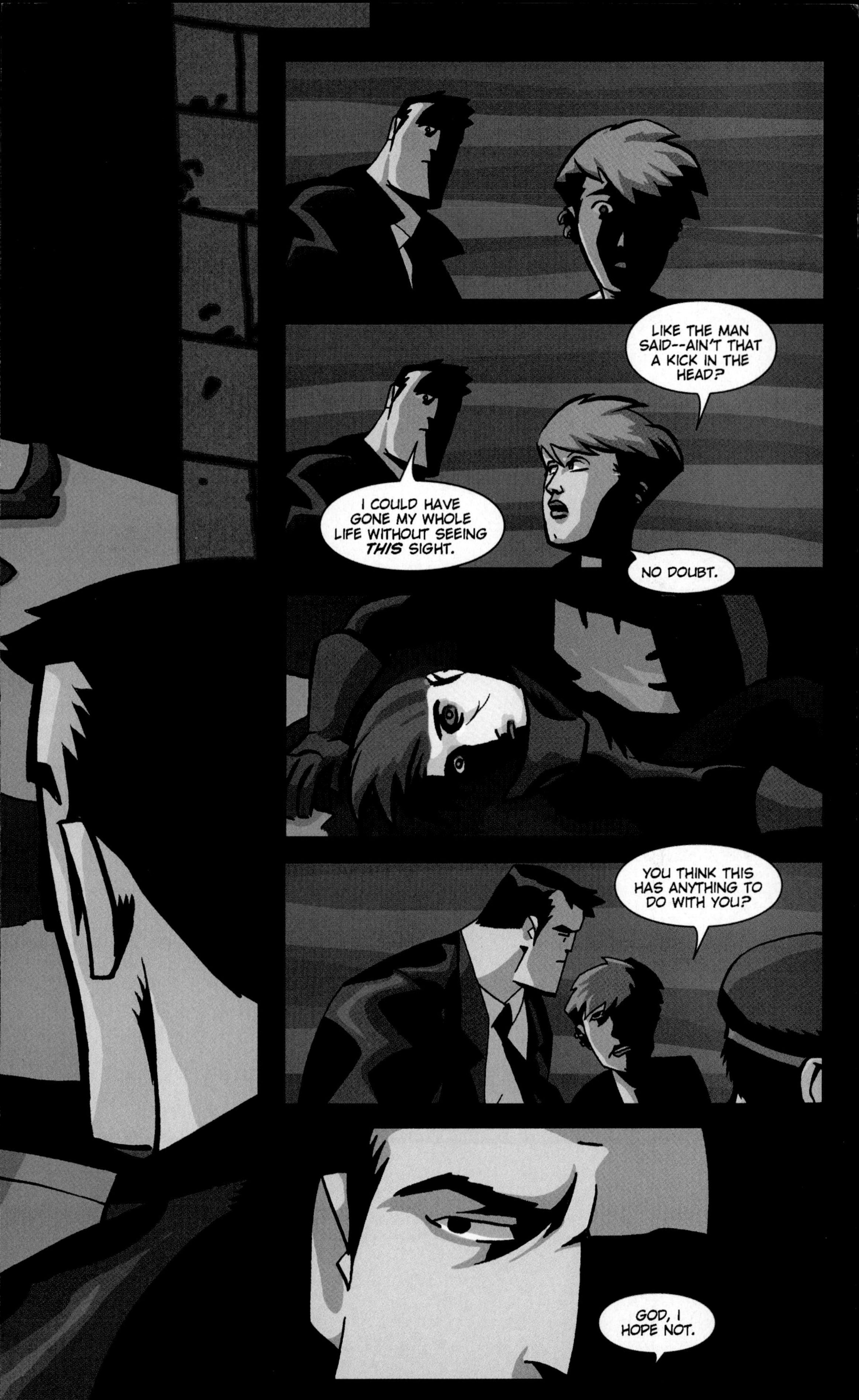
LIKE THE MAN SAID--AIN'T THAT A KICK IN THE HEAD?
I COULD HAVE GONE MY WHOLE LIFE WITHOUT SEEING *THIS* SIGHT.
NO DOUBT.
YOU THINK THIS HAS ANYTHING TO DO WITH YOU?
GOD, I HOPE NOT.

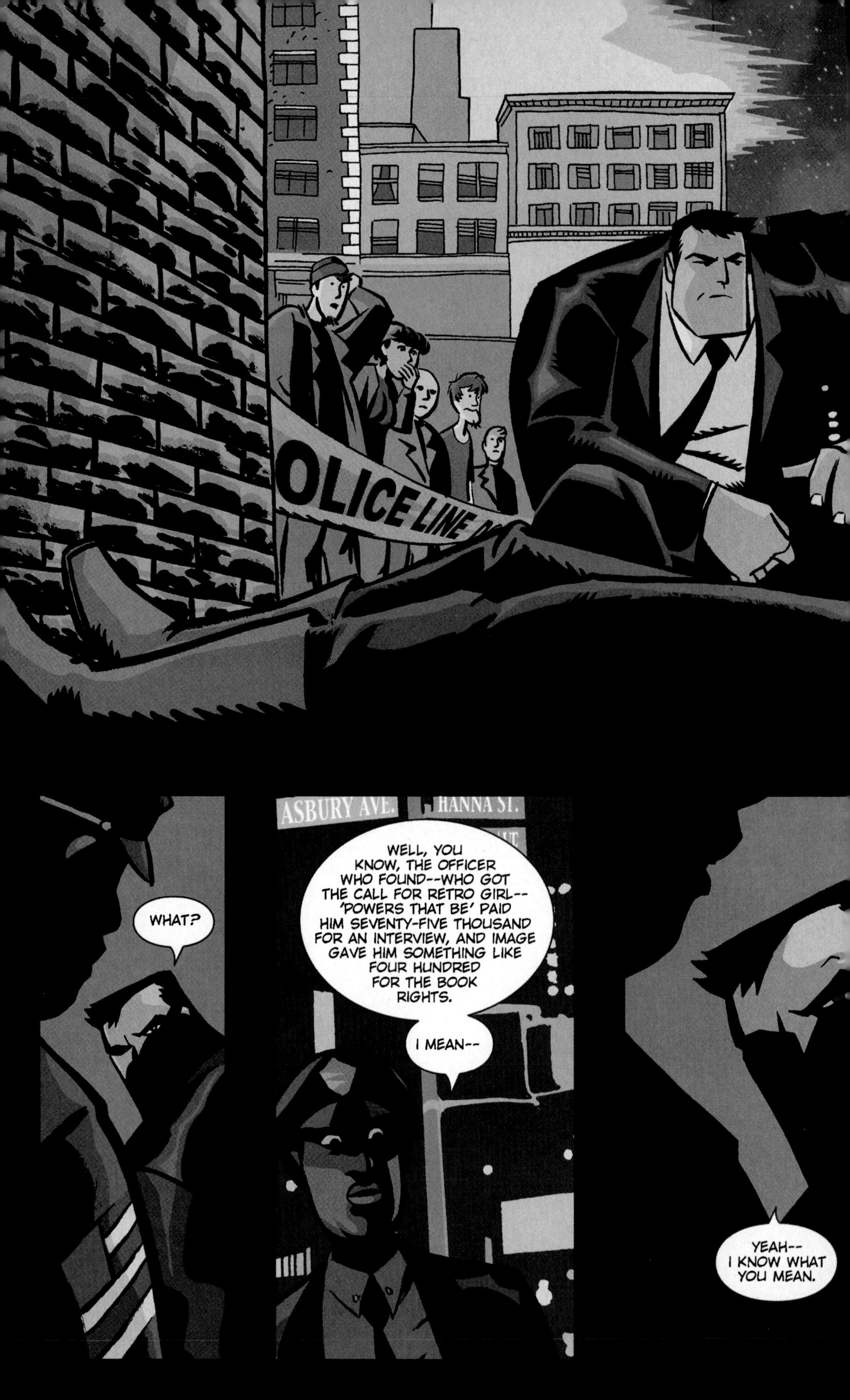
OLICE LINE D
ASBURY AVE.
HANNA ST.
WHAT?
WELL, YOU KNOW, THE OFFICER WHO FOUND--WHO GOT THE CALL FOR RETRO GIRL-- 'POWERS THAT BE' PAID HIM SEVENTY-FIVE THOUSAND FOR AN INTERVIEW, AND IMAGE GAVE HIM SOMETHING LIKE FOUR HUNDRED FOR THE BOOK RIGHTS.
I MEAN--
YEAH-- I KNOW WHAT YOU MEAN.

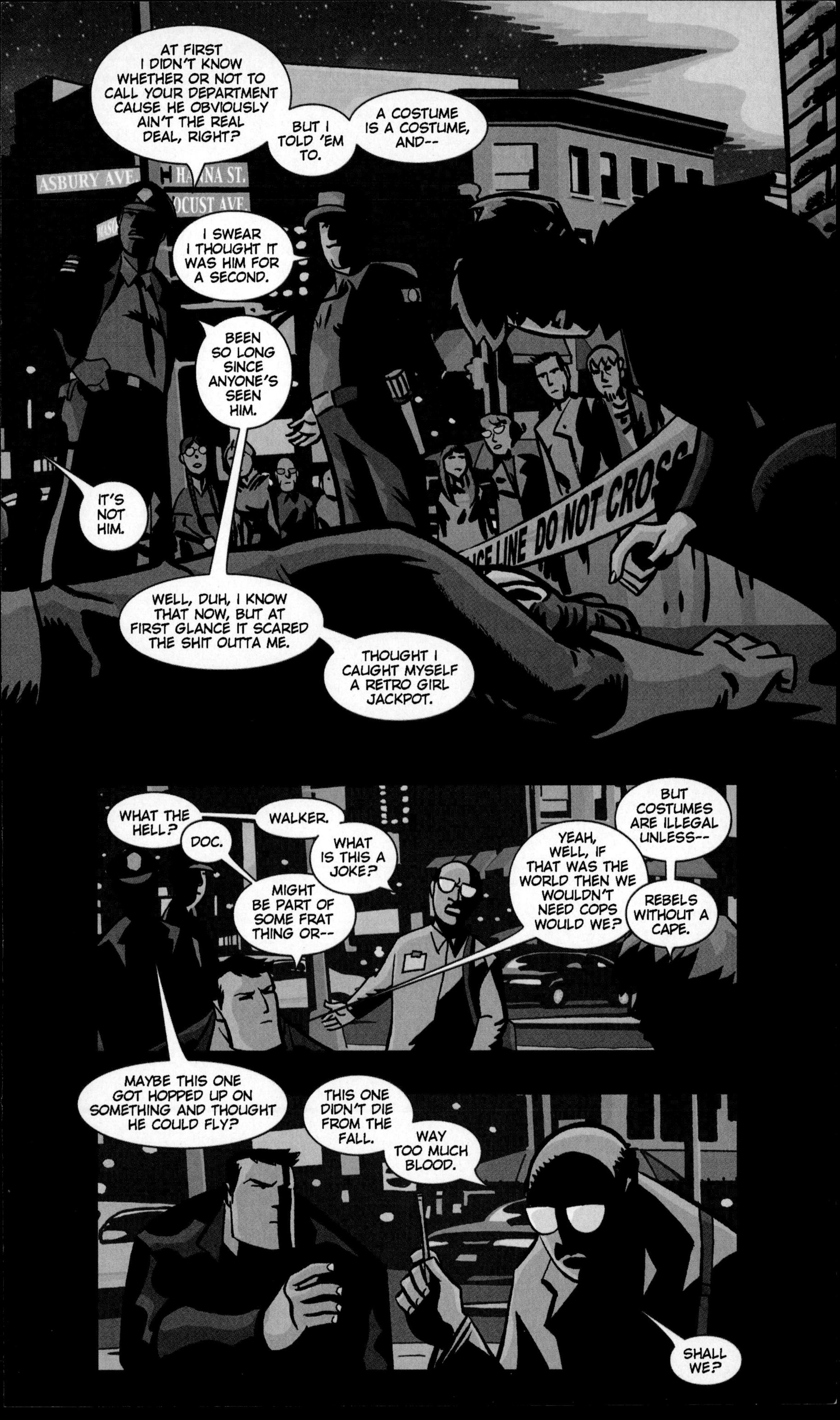
AT FIRST I DIDN'T KNOW WHETHER OR NOT TO CALL YOUR DEPARTMENT CAUSE HE OBVIOUSLY AIN'T THE REAL DEAL, RIGHT?
BUT I TOLD 'EM TO.
A COSTUME IS A COSTUME, AND--
ASBURY AVE.
HANNA ST.
LOCUST AVE.
I SWEAR I THOUGHT IT WAS HIM FOR A SECOND.
BEEN SO LONG SINCE ANYONE'S SEEN HIM.
IT'S NOT HIM.
DO NOT CROSS
WELL, DUH, I KNOW THAT NOW, BUT AT FIRST GLANCE IT SCARED THE SHIT OUTTA ME.
THOUGHT I CAUGHT MYSELF A RETRO GIRL JACKPOT.
WHAT THE HELL?
WALKER.
DOC.
WHAT IS THIS A JOKE?
MIGHT BE PART OF SOME FRAT THING OR--
YEAH, WELL, IF THAT WAS THE WORLD THEN WE WOULDN'T NEED COPS WOULD WE?
BUT COSTUMES ARE ILLEGAL UNLESS--
REBELS WITHOUT A CAPE.
MAYBE THIS ONE GOT HOPPED UP ON SOMETHING AND THOUGHT HE COULD FLY?
THIS ONE DIDN'T DIE FROM THE FALL.
WAY TOO MUCH BLOOD.
SHALL WE?

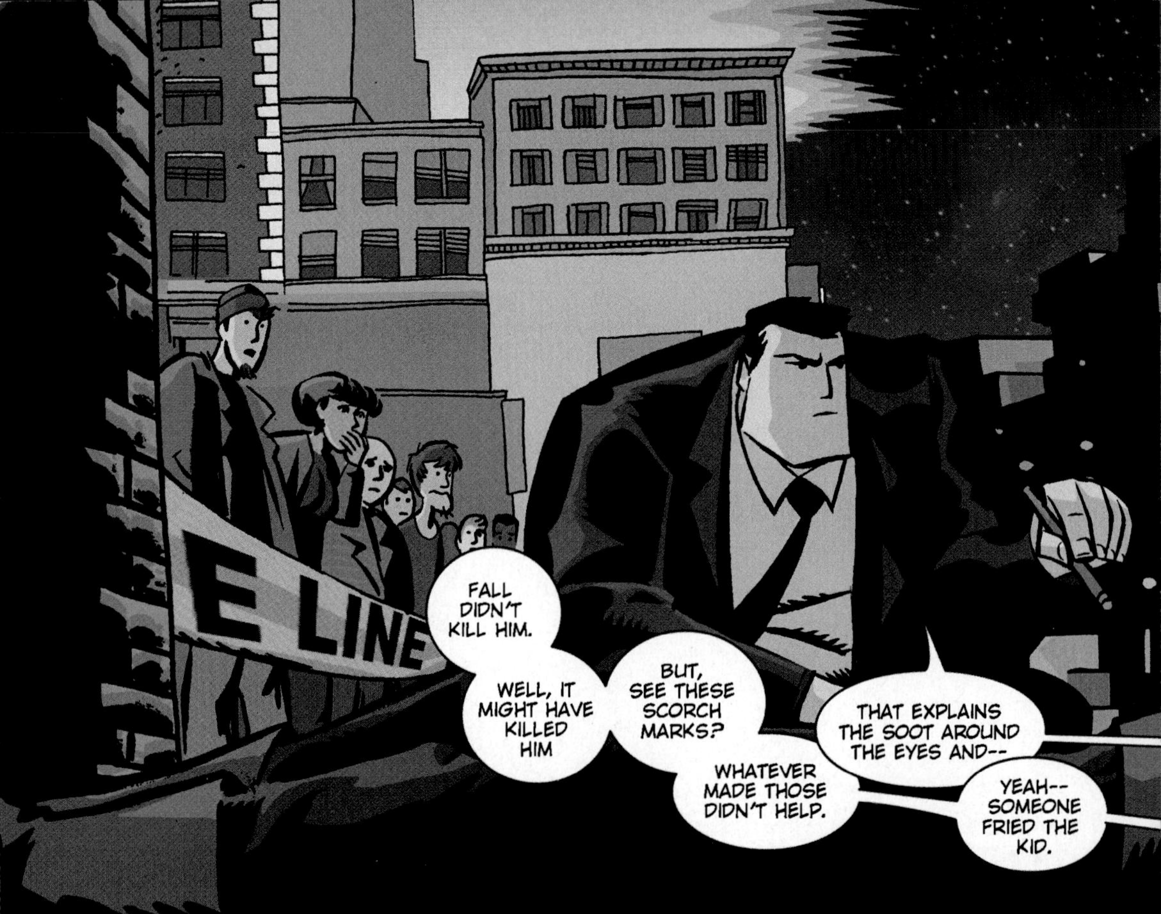
E LINE
FALL DIDN'T KILL HIM.
WELL, IT MIGHT HAVE KILLED HIM
BUT, SEE THESE SCORCH MARKS?
WHATEVER MADE THOSE DIDN'T HELP.
THAT EXPLAINS THE SOOT AROUND THE EYES AND--
YEAH-- SOMEONE FRIED THE KID.

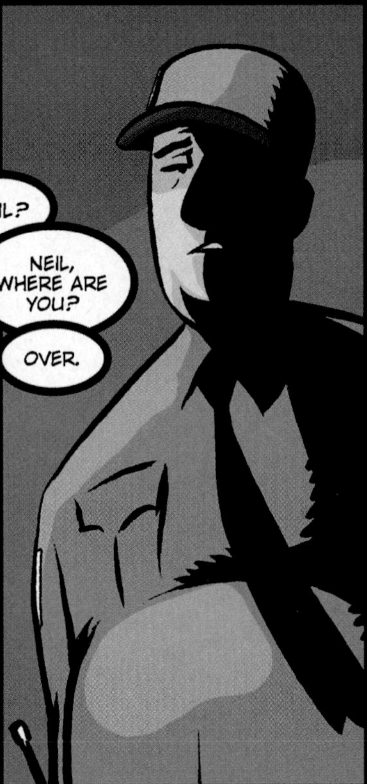
NEIL?
NEIL, WHERE ARE YOU?
OVER.

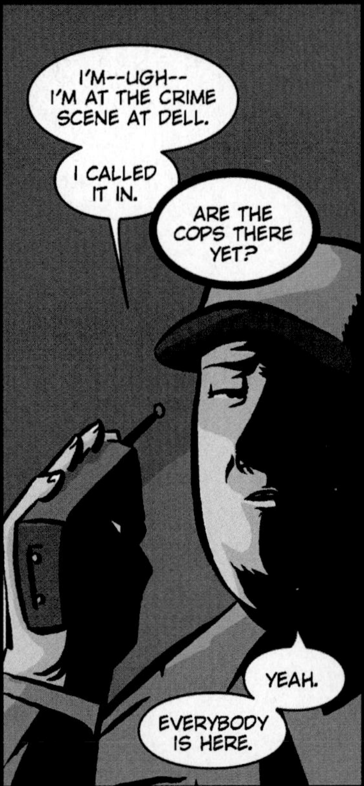
I'M--UGH-- I'M AT THE CRIME SCENE AT DELL.
I CALLED IT IN.
ARE THE COPS THERE YET?
YEAH.
EVERYBODY IS HERE.

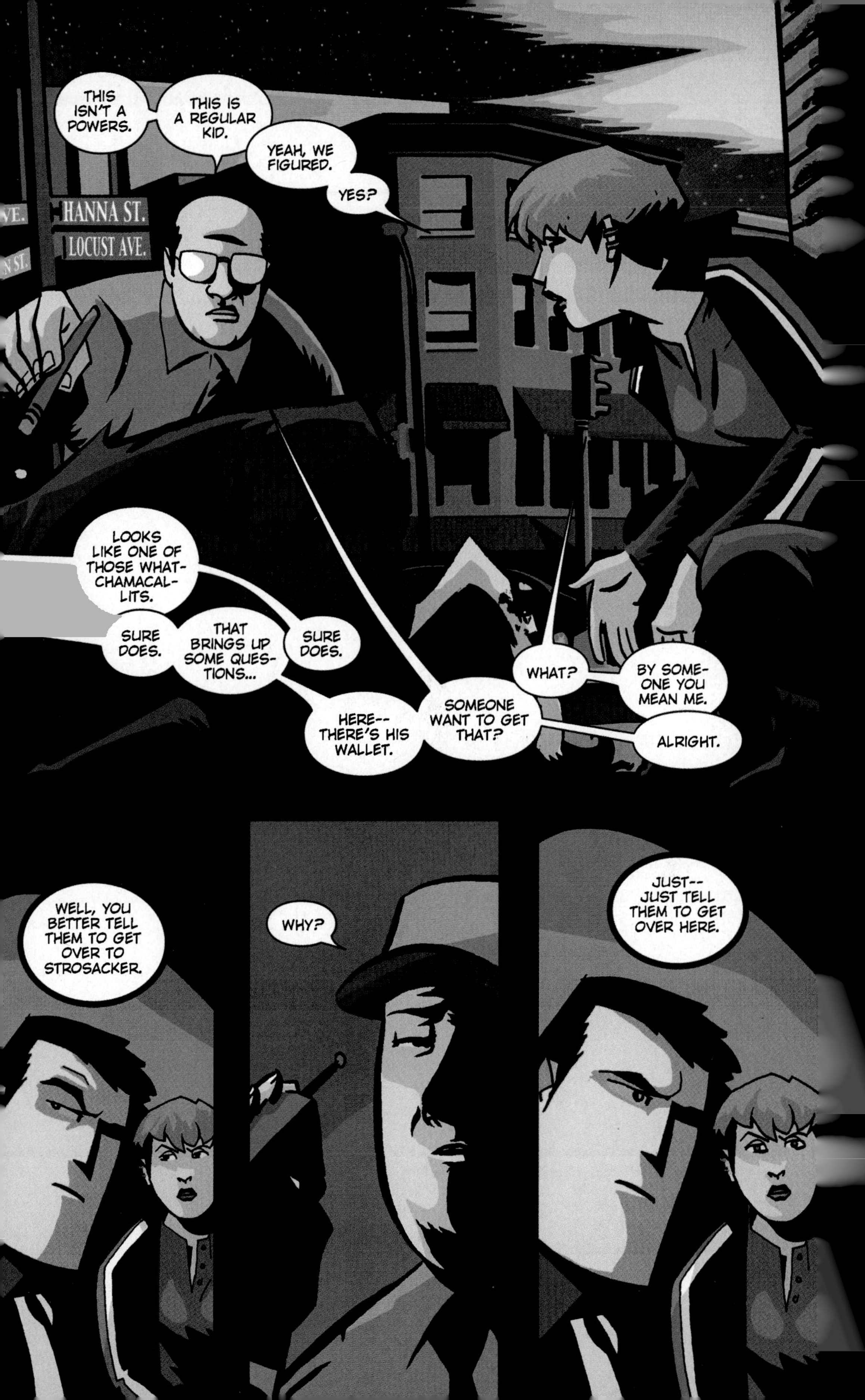
HANNA ST.
LOCUST AVE.
THIS ISN'T A POWERS.
THIS IS A REGULAR KID.
YEAH, WE FIGURED.
YES?
LOOKS LIKE ONE OF THOSE WHATCHAMACALLITS.
SURE DOES.
THAT BRINGS UP SOME QUESTIONS...
SURE DOES.
HERE-- THERE'S HIS WALLET.
SOMEONE WANT TO GET THAT?
WHAT?
BY SOMEONE YOU MEAN ME.
ALRIGHT.
WELL, YOU BETTER TELL THEM TO GET OVER TO STROSACKER.
WHY?
JUST-- JUST TELL THEM TO GET OVER HERE.

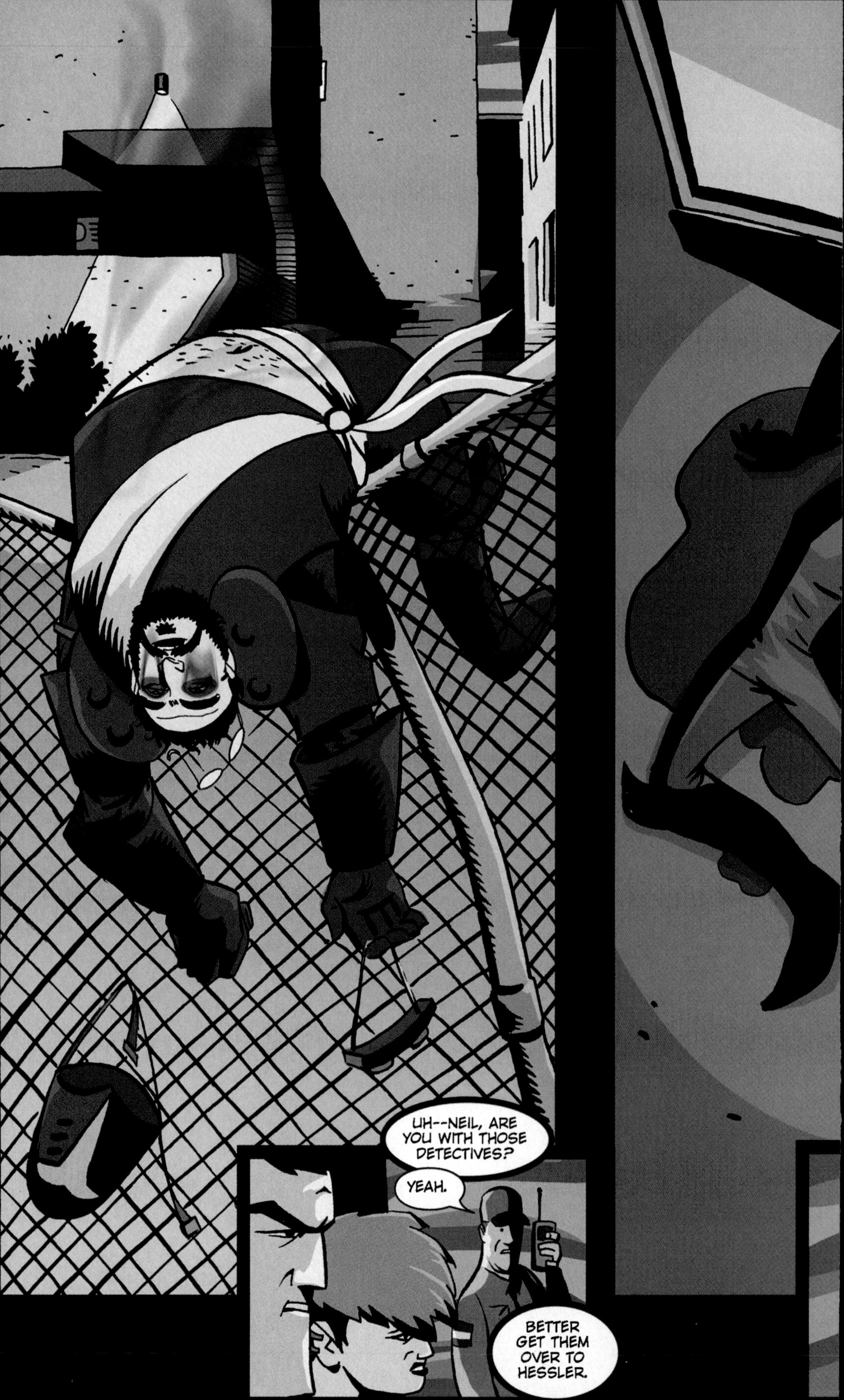
UH--NEIL, ARE YOU WITH THOSE DETECTIVES?
YEAH.
BETTER GET THEM OVER TO HESSLER.

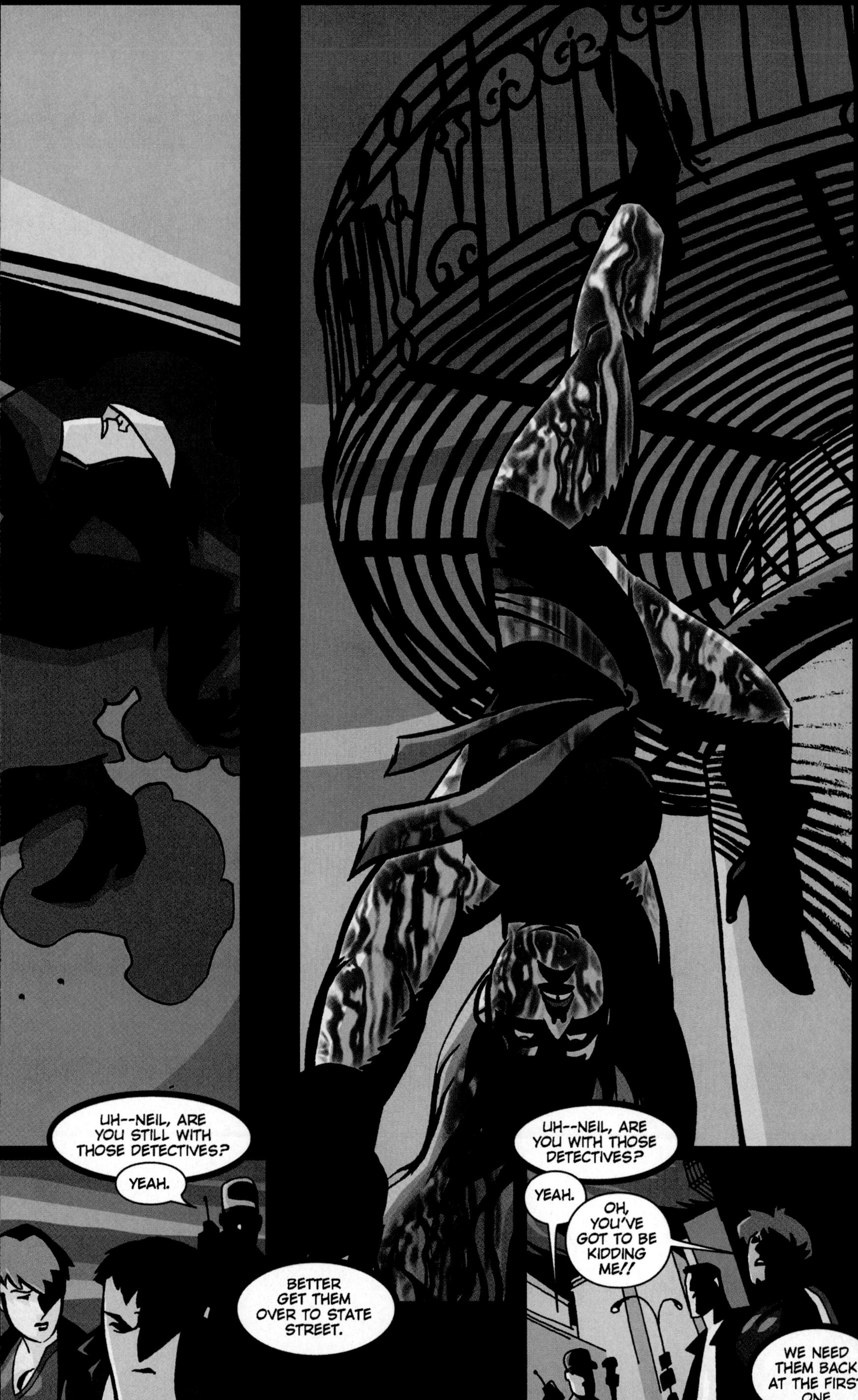
UH--NEIL, ARE YOU STILL WITH THOSE DETECTIVES?
YEAH.
BETTER GET THEM OVER TO STATE STREET.
UH--NEIL, ARE YOU WITH THOSE DETECTIVES?
YEAH.
OH, YOU'VE GOT TO BE KIDDING ME!!
WE NEED THEM BACK AT THE FIRST ONE

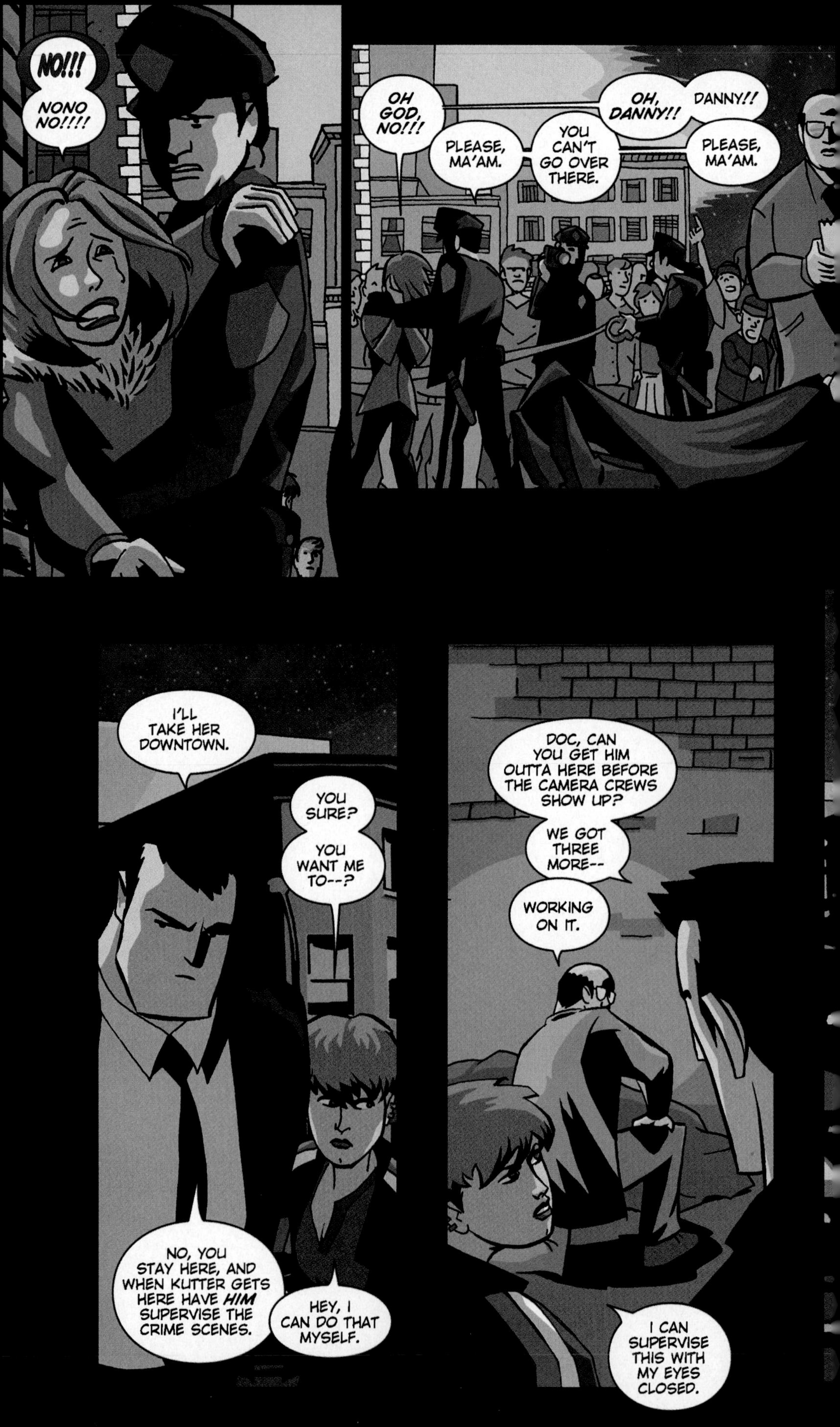
NO!!!
NONO NO!!!!
OH GOD, NO!!!
PLEASE, MA'AM.
YOU CAN'T GO OVER THERE.
OH, DANNY!!
DANNY!!
PLEASE, MA'AM.
I'LL TAKE HER DOWNTOWN.
YOU SURE?
YOU WANT ME TO--?
NO, YOU STAY HERE, AND WHEN KUTTER GETS HERE HAVE *HIM* SUPERVISE THE CRIME SCENES.
HEY, I CAN DO THAT MYSELF.
DOC, CAN YOU GET HIM OUTTA HERE BEFORE THE CAMERA CREWS SHOW UP?
WE GOT THREE MORE--
WORKING ON IT.
I CAN SUPERVISE THIS WITH MY EYES CLOSED.

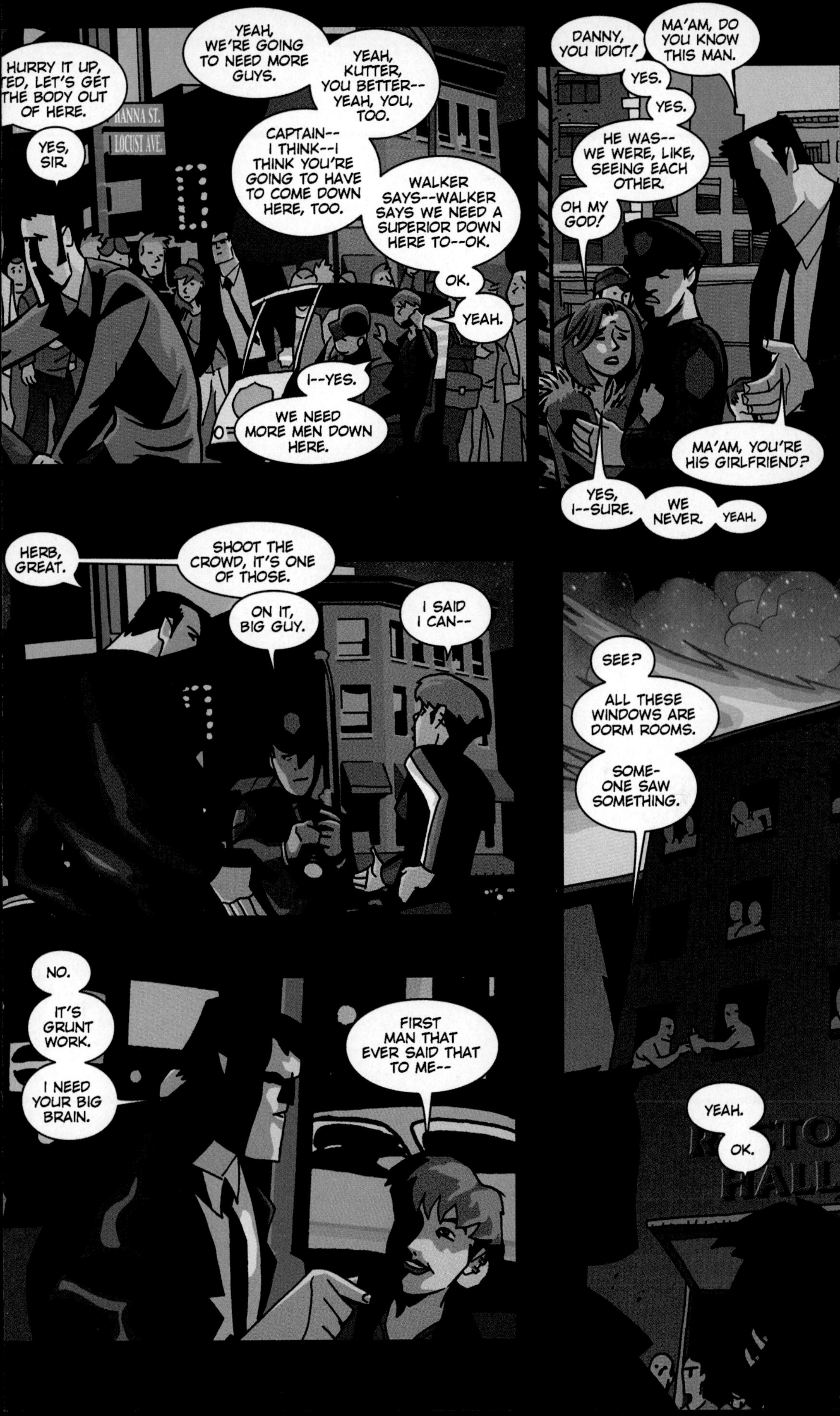
HURRY IT UP, TED, LET'S GET THE BODY OUT OF HERE.
HANNA ST.
LOCUST AVE.
YES, SIR.
YEAH, WE'RE GOING TO NEED MORE GUYS.
YEAH, KUTTER, YOU BETTER-- YEAH, YOU, TOO.
CAPTAIN-- I THINK--I THINK YOU'RE GOING TO HAVE TO COME DOWN HERE, TOO.
WALKER SAYS--WALKER SAYS WE NEED A SUPERIOR DOWN HERE TO--OK.
OK.
YEAH.
I--YES.
WE NEED MORE MEN DOWN HERE.
DANNY, YOU IDIOT!
MA'AM, DO YOU KNOW THIS MAN.
YES.
YES.
HE WAS-- WE WERE, LIKE, SEEING EACH OTHER.
OH MY GOD!
MA'AM, YOU'RE HIS GIRLFRIEND?
YES, I--SURE.
WE NEVER.
YEAH.
HERB, GREAT.
SHOOT THE CROWD, IT'S ONE OF THOSE.
ON IT, BIG GUY.
I SAID I CAN--
NO.
IT'S GRUNT WORK.
I NEED YOUR BIG BRAIN.
FIRST MAN THAT EVER SAID THAT TO ME--
SEE?
ALL THESE WINDOWS ARE DORM ROOMS.
SOME-ONE SAW SOMETHING.
YEAH.
OK.

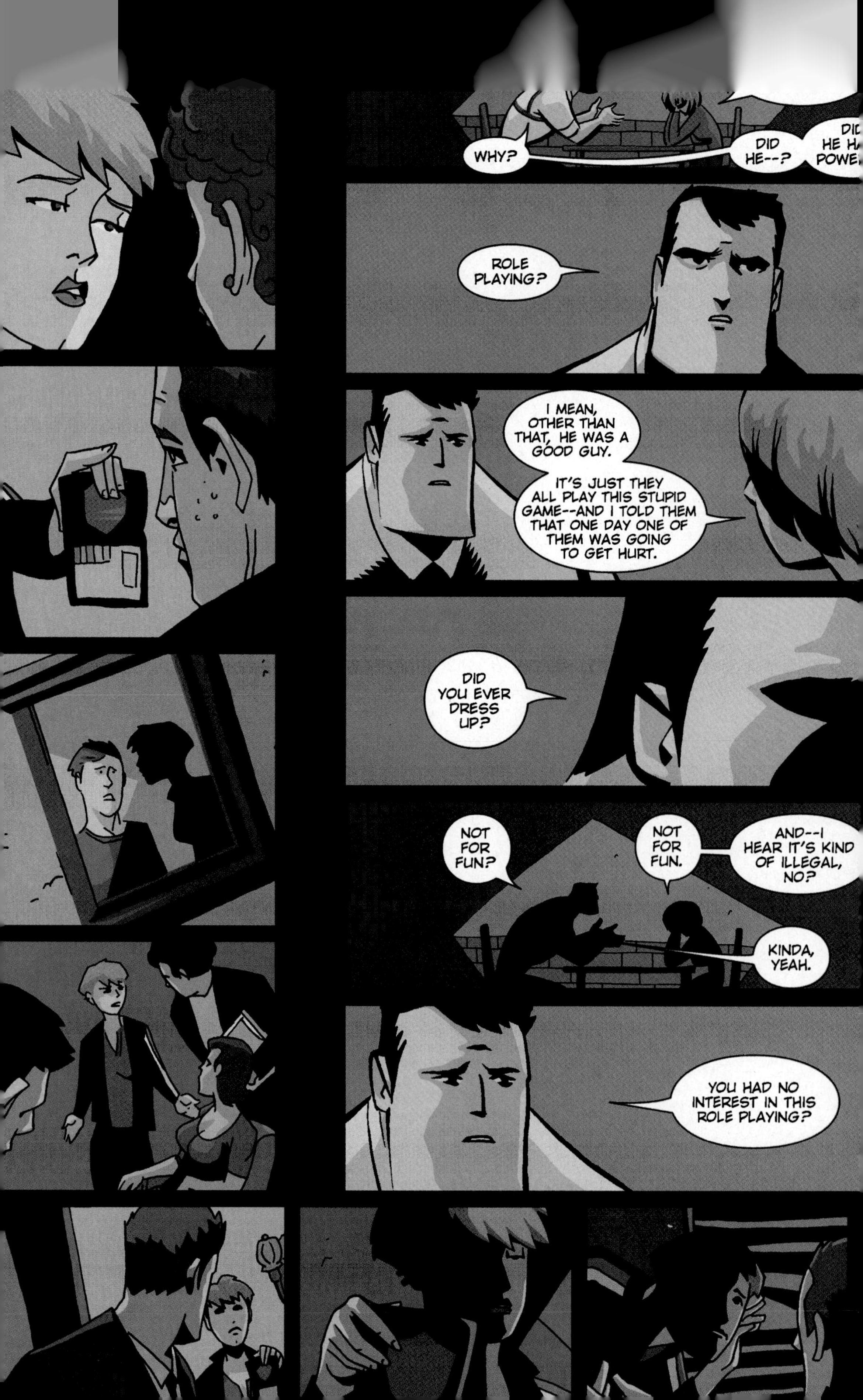
WHY?
DID HE--?
ROLE PLAYING?
I MEAN, OTHER THAN THAT, HE WAS A GOOD GUY.
IT'S JUST THEY ALL PLAY THIS STUPID GAME--AND I TOLD THEM THAT ONE DAY ONE OF THEM WAS GOING TO GET HURT.
DID YOU EVER DRESS UP?
NOT FOR FUN?
NOT FOR FUN.
AND--I HEAR IT'S KIND OF ILLEGAL, NO?
KINDA, YEAH.
YOU HAD NO INTEREST IN THIS ROLE PLAYING?

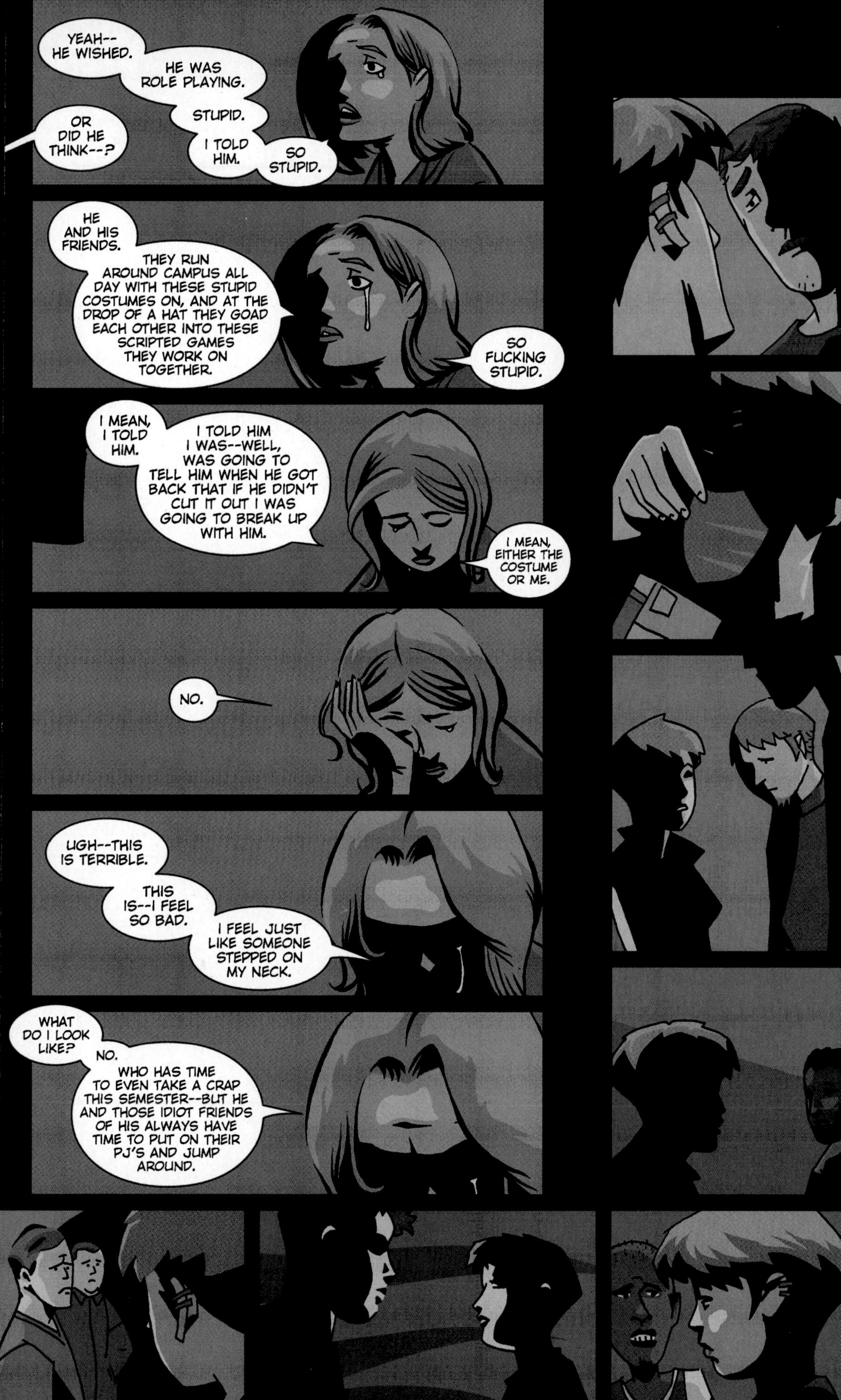
YEAH--
HE WISHED.
HE WAS ROLE PLAYING.
STUPID.
OR DID HE THINK--?
I TOLD HIM.
SO STUPID.
HE AND HIS FRIENDS.
THEY RUN AROUND CAMPUS ALL DAY WITH THESE STUPID COSTUMES ON, AND AT THE DROP OF A HAT THEY GOAD EACH OTHER INTO THESE SCRIPTED GAMES THEY WORK ON TOGETHER.
SO FUCKING STUPID.
I MEAN, I TOLD HIM.
I TOLD HIM I WAS--WELL, WAS GOING TO TELL HIM WHEN HE GOT BACK THAT IF HE DIDN'T CUT IT OUT I WAS GOING TO BREAK UP WITH HIM.
I MEAN, EITHER THE COSTUME OR ME.
NO.
UGH--THIS IS TERRIBLE.
THIS IS--I FEEL SO BAD.
I FEEL JUST LIKE SOMEONE STEPPED ON MY NECK.
WHAT DO I LOOK LIKE?
NO.
WHO HAS TIME TO EVEN TAKE A CRAP THIS SEMESTER--BUT HE AND THOSE IDIOT FRIENDS OF HIS ALWAYS HAVE TIME TO PUT ON THEIR PJ'S AND JUMP AROUND.

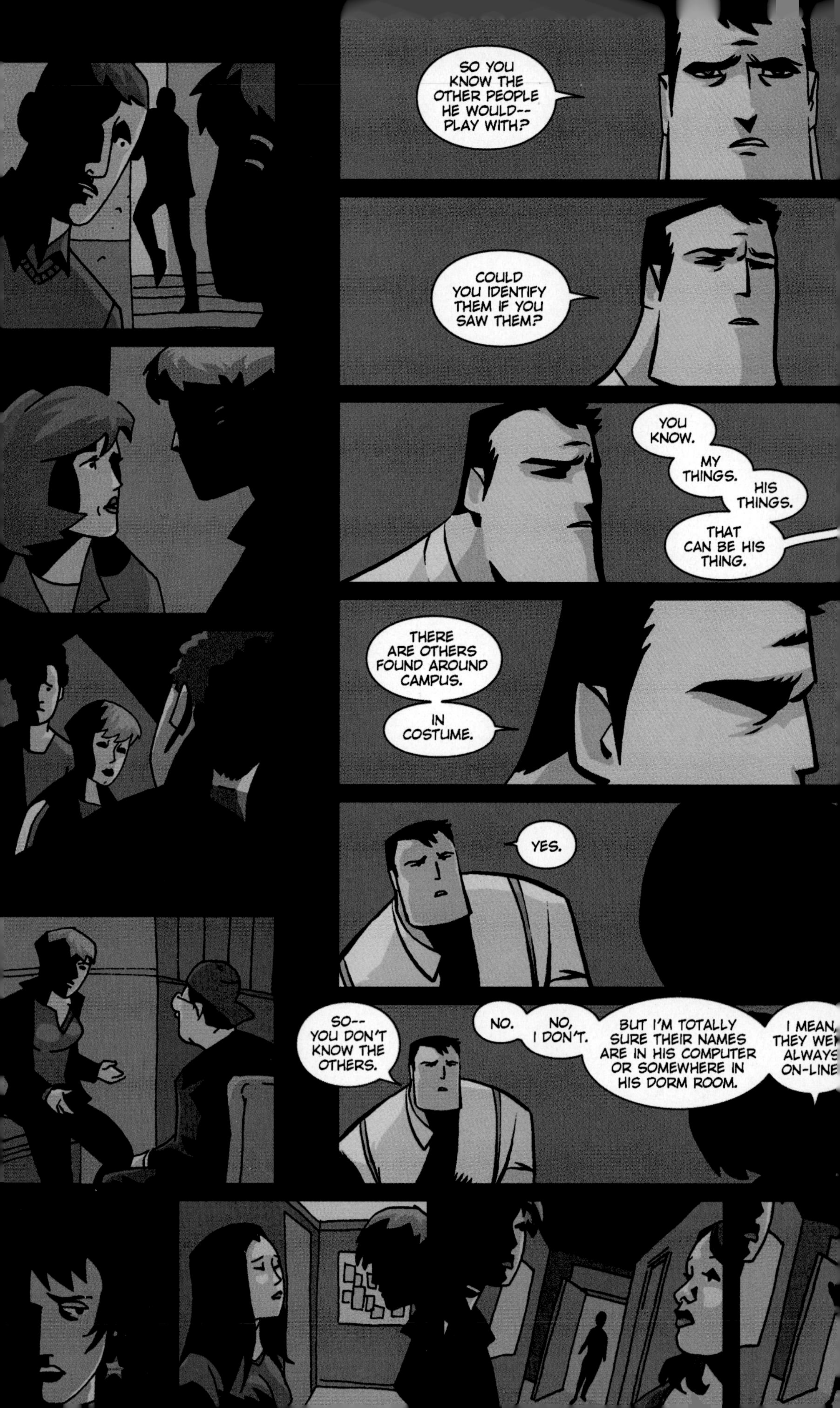

SO YOU KNOW THE OTHER PEOPLE HE WOULD-- PLAY WITH?
COULD YOU IDENTIFY THEM IF YOU SAW THEM?
YOU KNOW.
MY THINGS.
HIS THINGS.
THAT CAN BE HIS THING.
THERE ARE OTHERS FOUND AROUND CAMPUS.
IN COSTUME.
YES.
SO-- YOU DON'T KNOW THE OTHERS.
NO.
NO, I DON'T.
BUT I'M TOTALLY SURE THEIR NAMES ARE IN HIS COMPUTER OR SOMEWHERE IN HIS DORM ROOM.

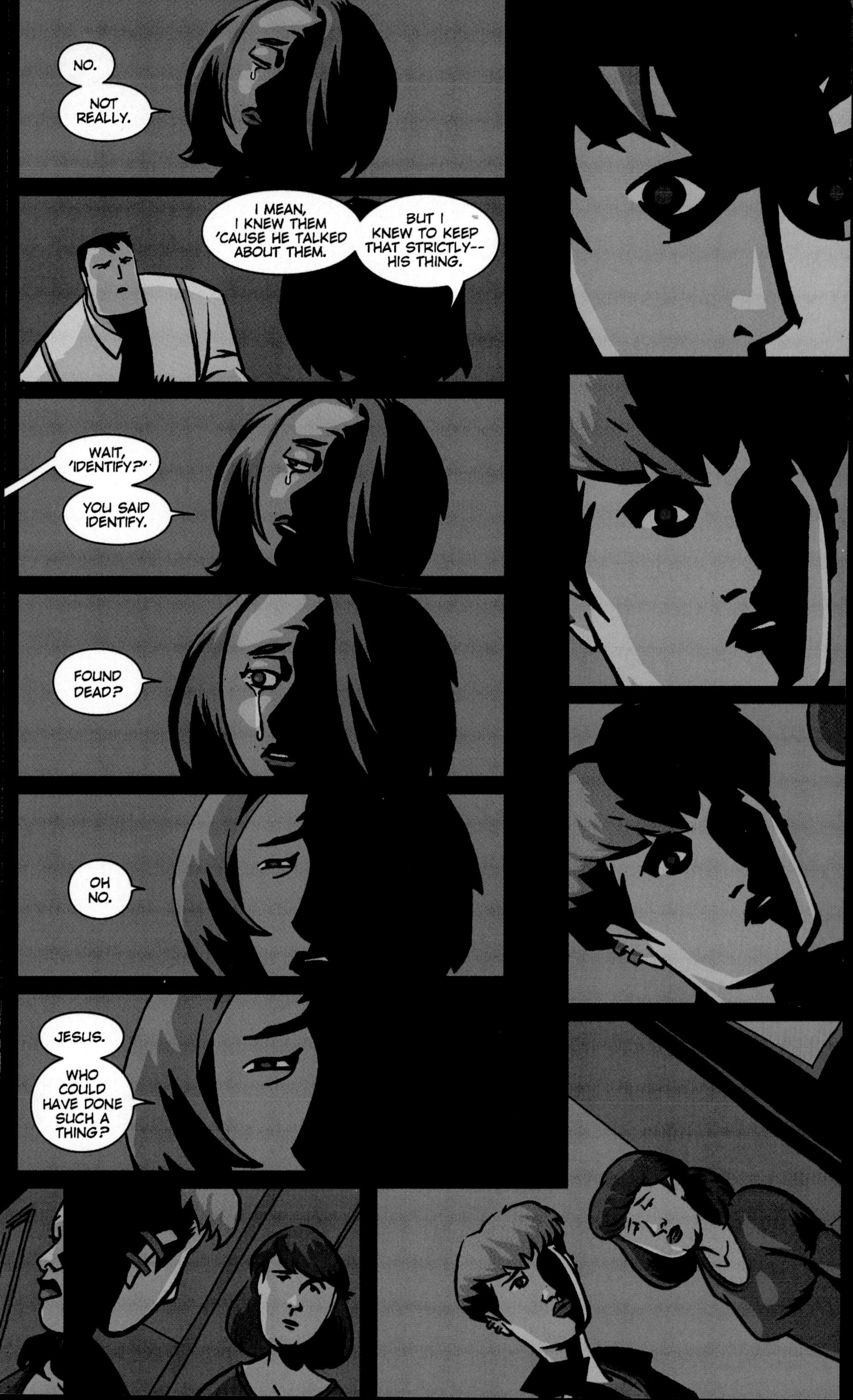
NO.
NOT REALLY.
I MEAN, I KNEW THEM 'CAUSE HE TALKED ABOUT THEM.
BUT I KNEW TO KEEP THAT STRICTLY-- HIS THING.
WAIT, 'IDENTIFY?'
YOU SAID IDENTIFY.
FOUND DEAD?
OH NO.
JESUS.
WHO COULD HAVE DONE SUCH A THING?

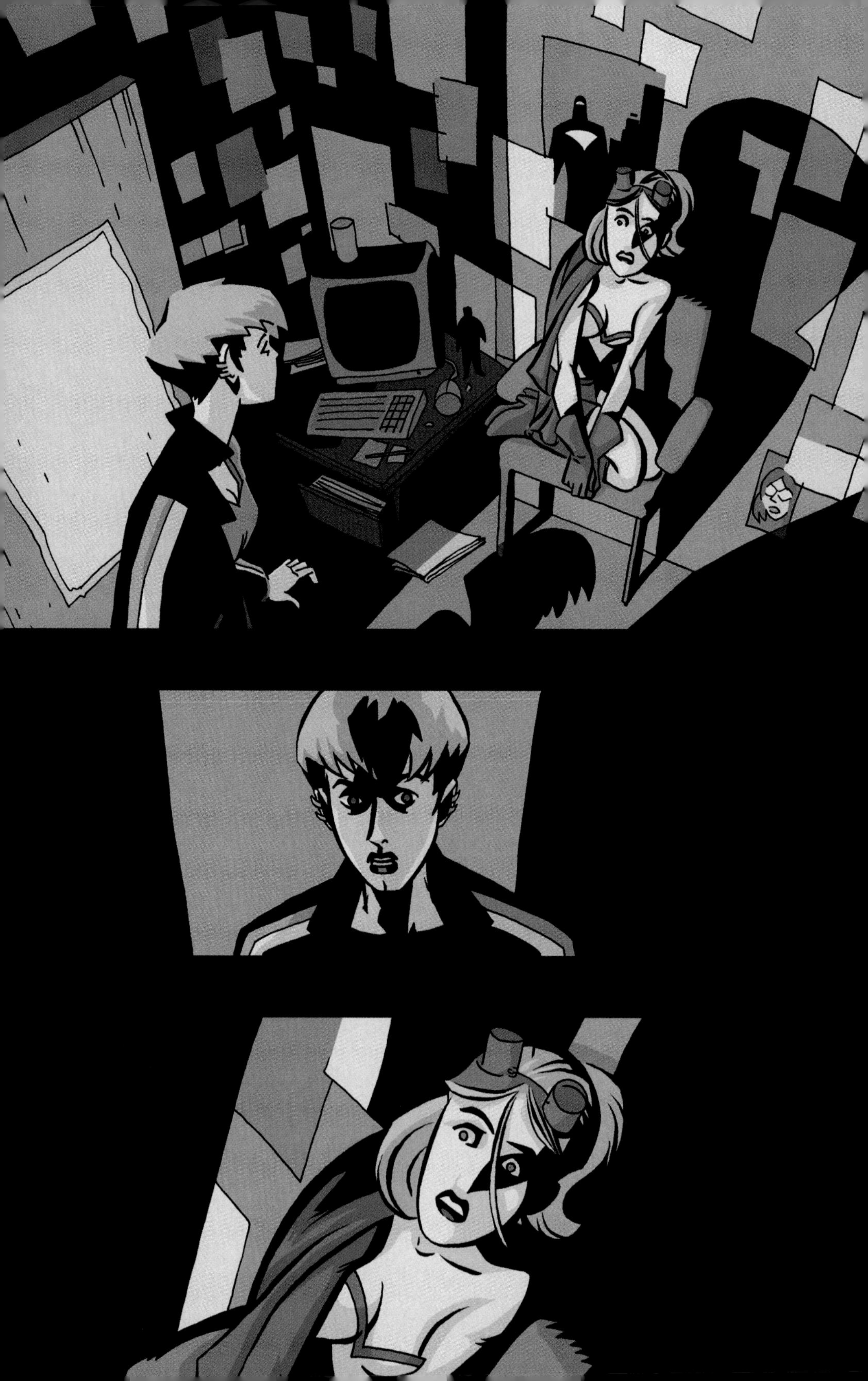

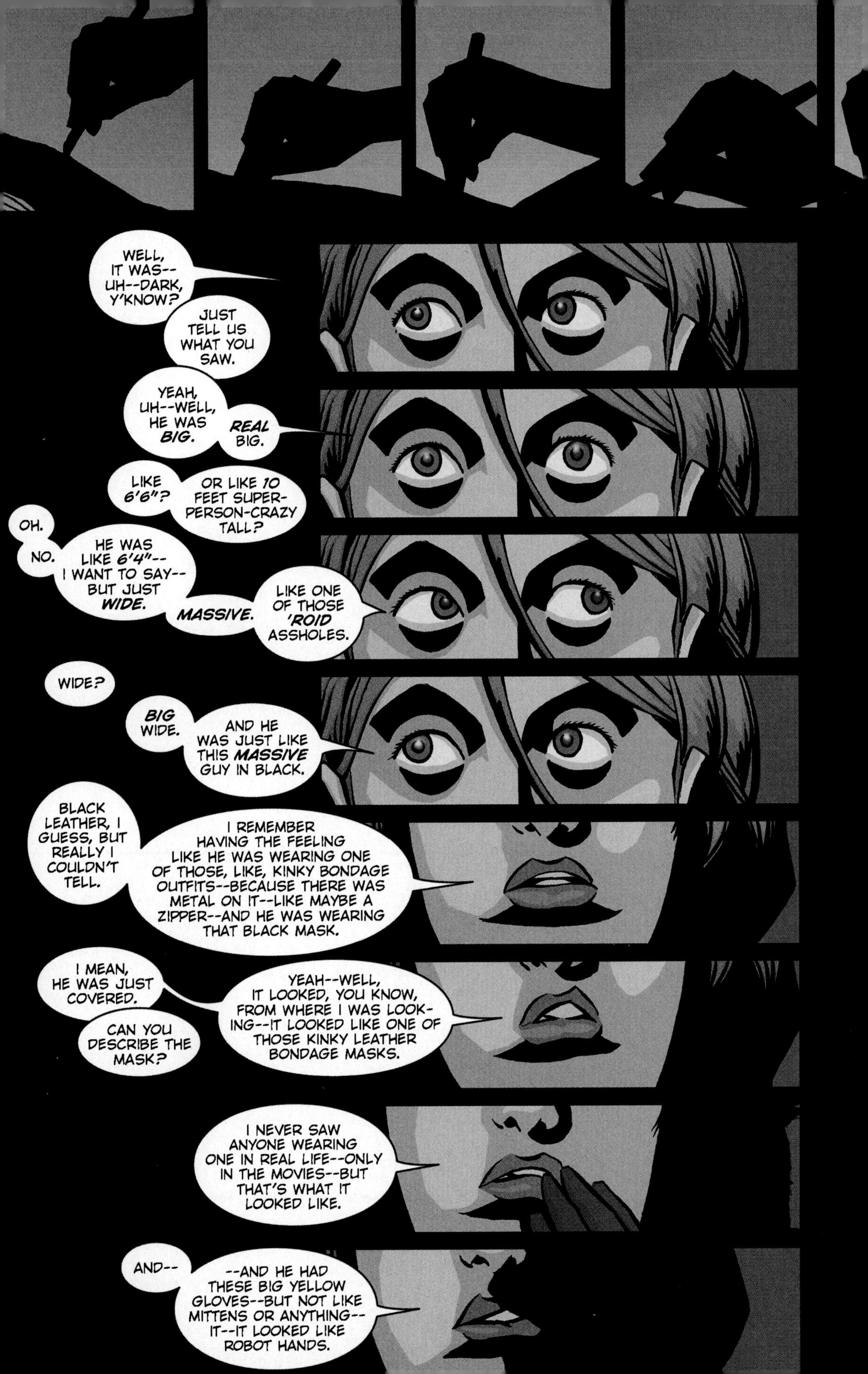
WELL, IT WAS--UH--DARK, Y'KNOW?
JUST TELL US WHAT YOU SAW.
YEAH, UH--WELL, HE WAS BIG.
REAL BIG.
LIKE 6'6"?
OR LIKE 10 FEET SUPER-PERSON-CRAZY TALL?
OH.
NO.
HE WAS LIKE 6'4"--I WANT TO SAY--BUT JUST WIDE.
MASSIVE.
LIKE ONE OF THOSE 'ROID ASSHOLES.
WIDE?
BIG WIDE.
AND HE WAS JUST LIKE THIS MASSIVE GUY IN BLACK.
BLACK LEATHER, I GUESS, BUT REALLY I COULDN'T TELL.
I REMEMBER HAVING THE FEELING LIKE HE WAS WEARING ONE OF THOSE, LIKE, KINKY BONDAGE OUTFITS--BECAUSE THERE WAS METAL ON IT--LIKE MAYBE A ZIPPER--AND HE WAS WEARING THAT BLACK MASK.
I MEAN, HE WAS JUST COVERED.
CAN YOU DESCRIBE THE MASK?
YEAH--WELL, IT LOOKED, YOU KNOW, FROM WHERE I WAS LOOKING--IT LOOKED LIKE ONE OF THOSE KINKY LEATHER BONDAGE MASKS.
I NEVER SAW ANYONE WEARING ONE IN REAL LIFE--ONLY IN THE MOVIES--BUT THAT'S WHAT IT LOOKED LIKE.
AND--
--AND HE HAD THESE BIG YELLOW GLOVES--BUT NOT LIKE MITTENS OR ANYTHING--IT--IT LOOKED LIKE ROBOT HANDS.

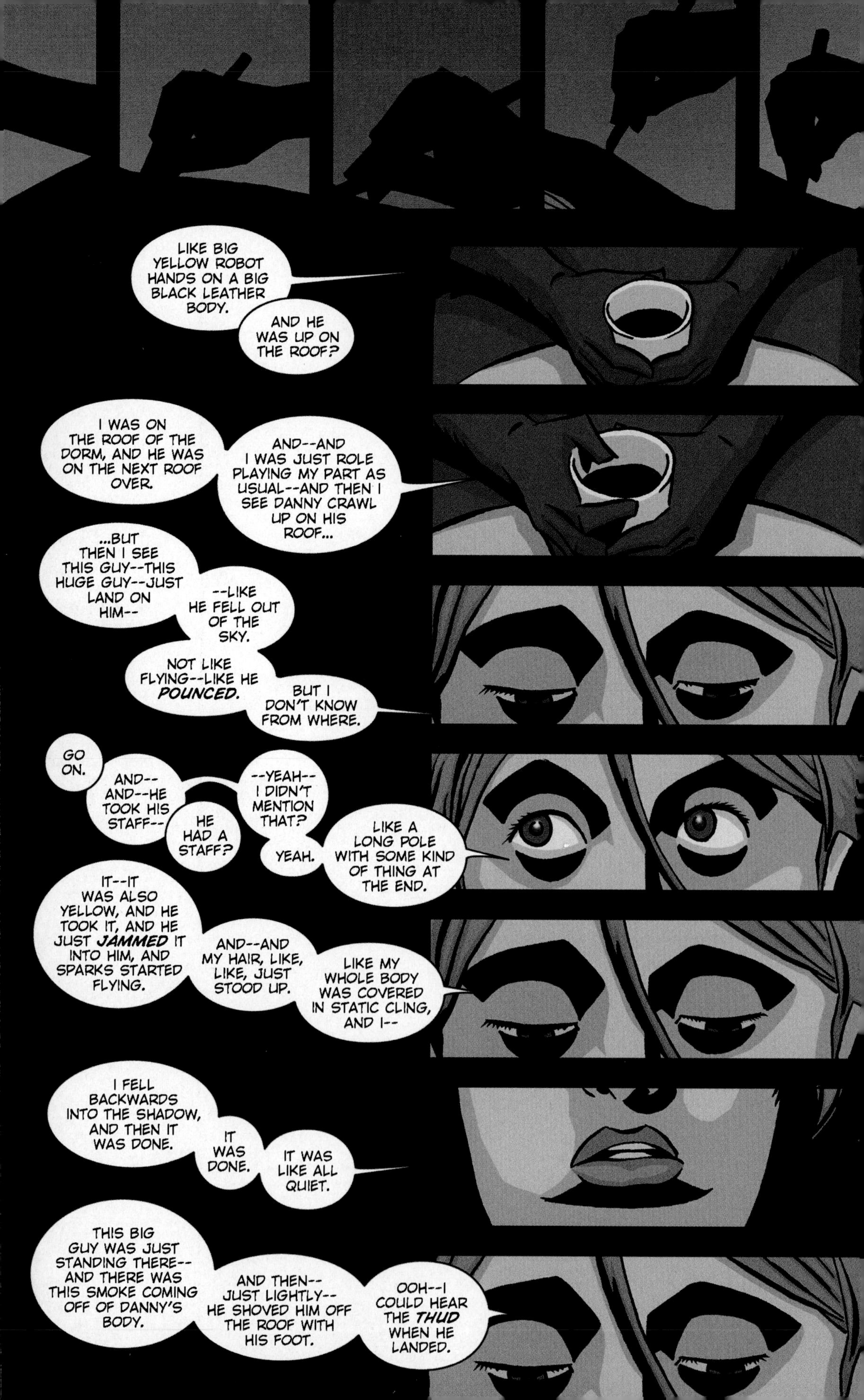
LIKE BIG YELLOW ROBOT HANDS ON A BIG BLACK LEATHER BODY.
AND HE WAS UP ON THE ROOF?
I WAS ON THE ROOF OF THE DORM, AND HE WAS ON THE NEXT ROOF OVER.
AND--AND I WAS JUST ROLE PLAYING MY PART AS USUAL--AND THEN I SEE DANNY CRAWL UP ON HIS ROOF...
...BUT THEN I SEE THIS GUY--THIS HUGE GUY--JUST LAND ON HIM--
--LIKE HE FELL OUT OF THE SKY.
NOT LIKE FLYING--LIKE HE *POUNCED.*
BUT I DON'T KNOW FROM WHERE.
GO ON.
AND--AND--HE TOOK HIS STAFF--
HE HAD A STAFF?
--YEAH--I DIDN'T MENTION THAT?
YEAH.
LIKE A LONG POLE WITH SOME KIND OF THING AT THE END.
IT--IT WAS ALSO YELLOW, AND HE TOOK IT, AND HE JUST *JAMMED* IT INTO HIM, AND SPARKS STARTED FLYING.
AND--AND MY HAIR, LIKE, LIKE, JUST STOOD UP.
LIKE MY WHOLE BODY WAS COVERED IN STATIC CLING, AND I--
I FELL BACKWARDS INTO THE SHADOW, AND THEN IT WAS DONE.
IT WAS DONE.
IT WAS LIKE ALL QUIET.
THIS BIG GUY WAS JUST STANDING THERE--AND THERE WAS THIS SMOKE COMING OFF OF DANNY'S BODY.
AND THEN--JUST LIGHTLY--HE SHOVED HIM OFF THE ROOF WITH HIS FOOT.
OOH--I COULD HEAR THE *THUD* WHEN HE LANDED.

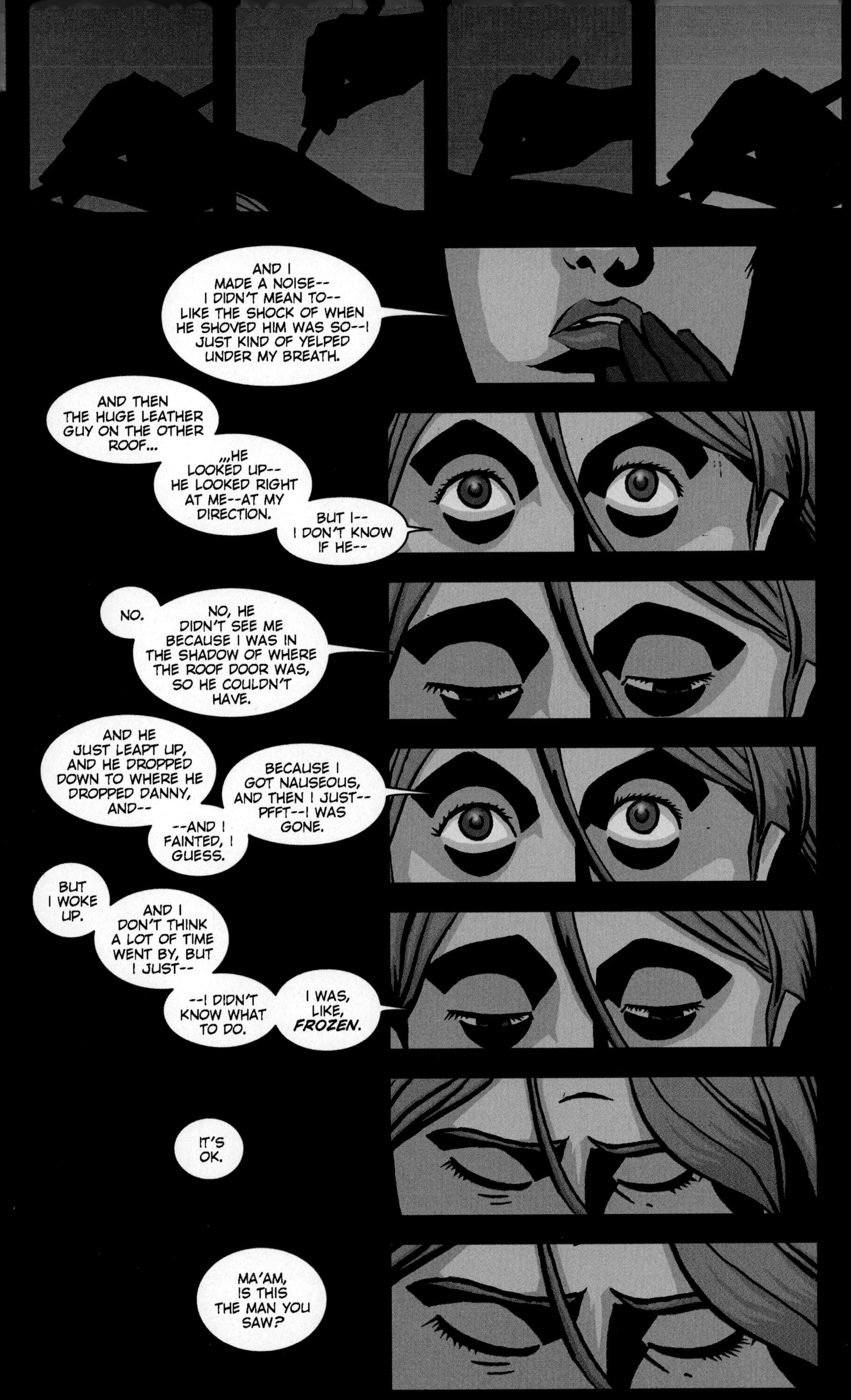

AND I MADE A NOISE-- I DIDN'T MEAN TO-- LIKE THE SHOCK OF WHEN HE SHOVED HIM WAS SO--I JUST KIND OF YELPED UNDER MY BREATH.
AND THEN THE HUGE LEATHER GUY ON THE OTHER ROOF...
...HE LOOKED UP-- HE LOOKED RIGHT AT ME--AT MY DIRECTION.
BUT I-- I DON'T KNOW IF HE--
NO.
NO, HE DIDN'T SEE ME BECAUSE I WAS IN THE SHADOW OF WHERE THE ROOF DOOR WAS, SO HE COULDN'T HAVE.
AND HE JUST LEAPT UP, AND HE DROPPED DOWN TO WHERE HE DROPPED DANNY, AND--
--AND I FAINTED, I GUESS.
BECAUSE I GOT NAUSEOUS, AND THEN I JUST-- PFFT--I WAS GONE.
BUT I WOKE UP.
AND I DON'T THINK A LOT OF TIME WENT BY, BUT I JUST--
--I DIDN'T KNOW WHAT TO DO.
I WAS, LIKE, *FROZEN*.
IT'S OK.
MA'AM, IS THIS THE MAN YOU SAW?

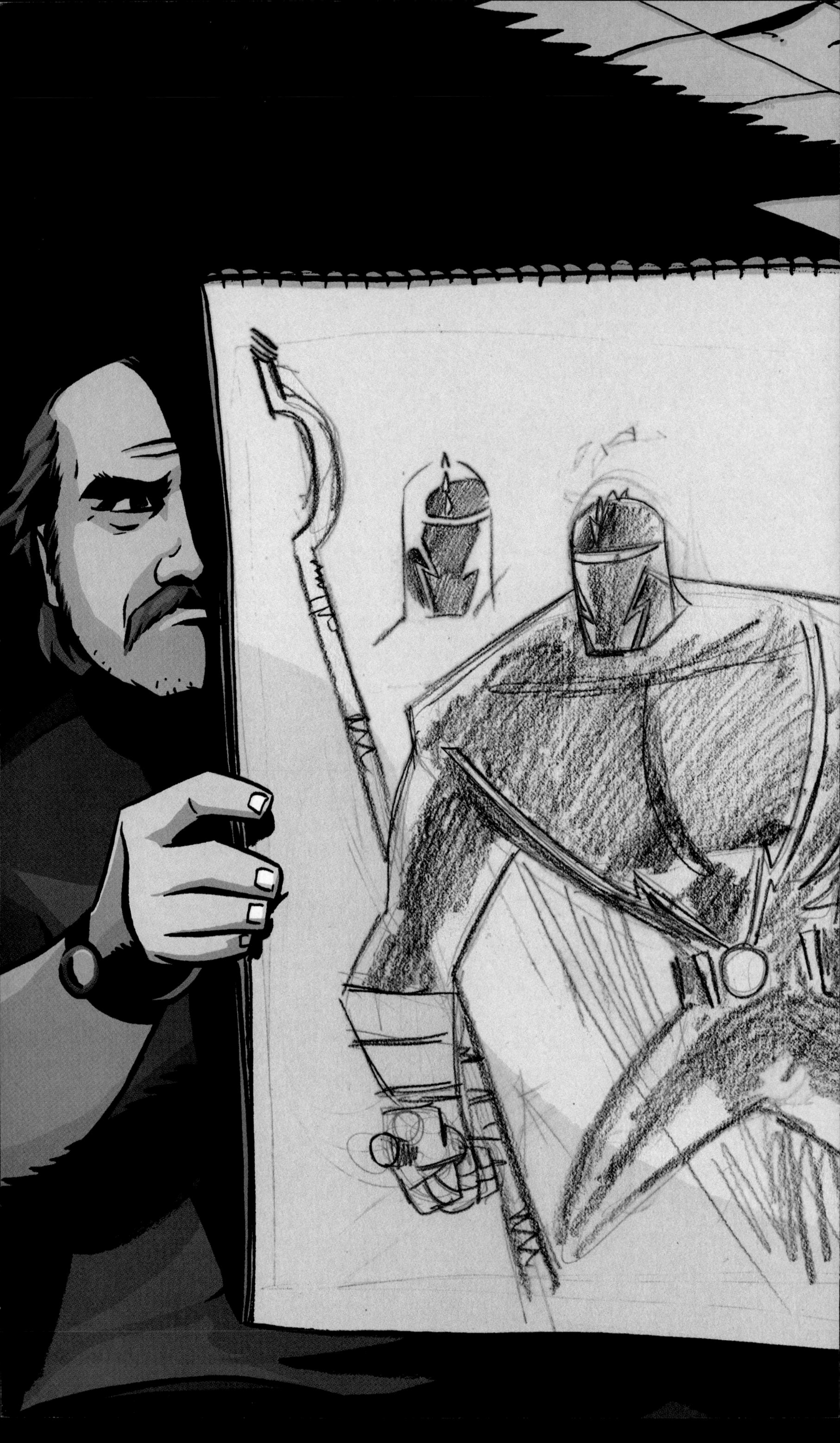

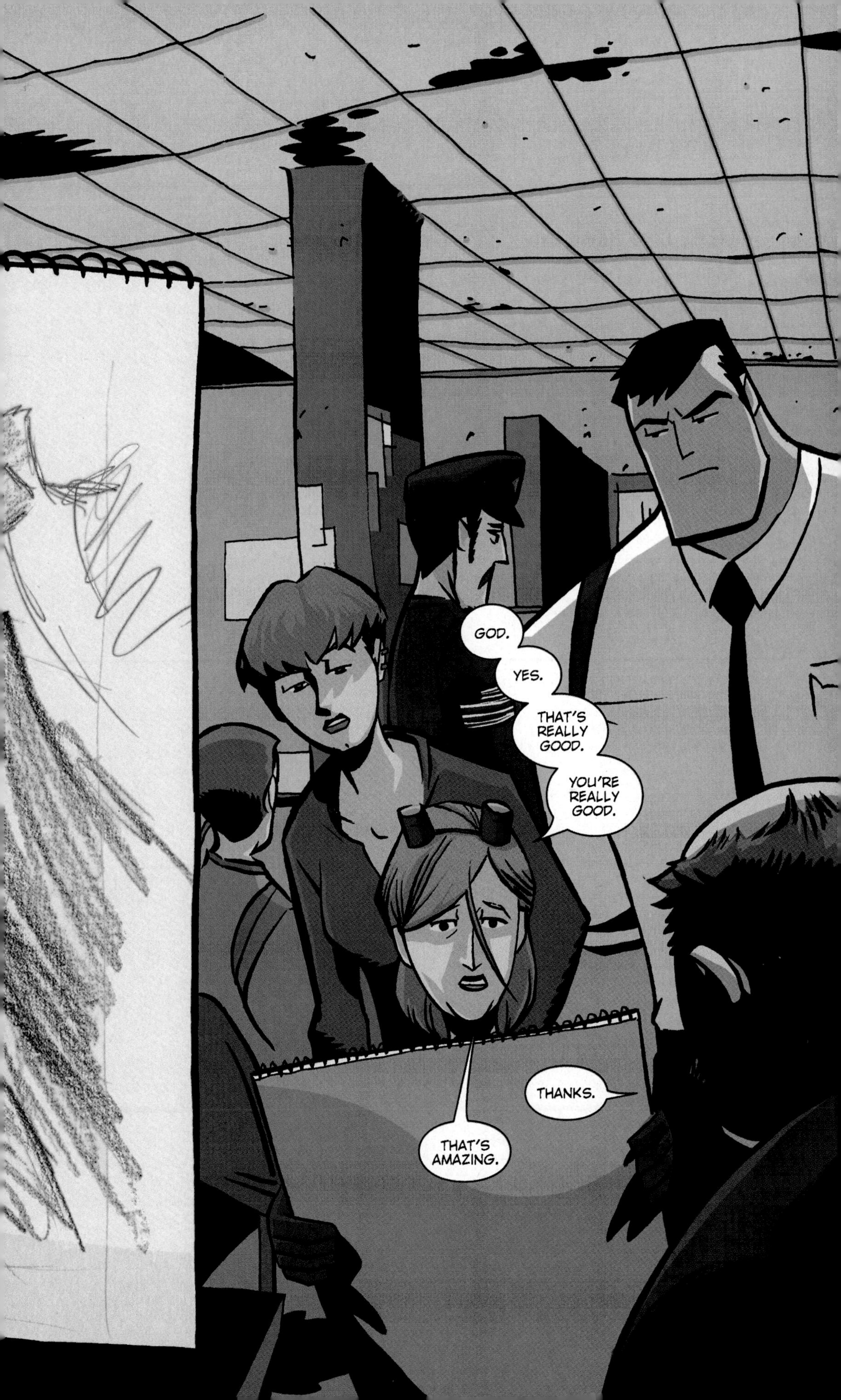
GOD.
YES.
THAT'S REALLY GOOD.
YOU'RE REALLY GOOD.
THAT'S AMAZING.
THANKS.

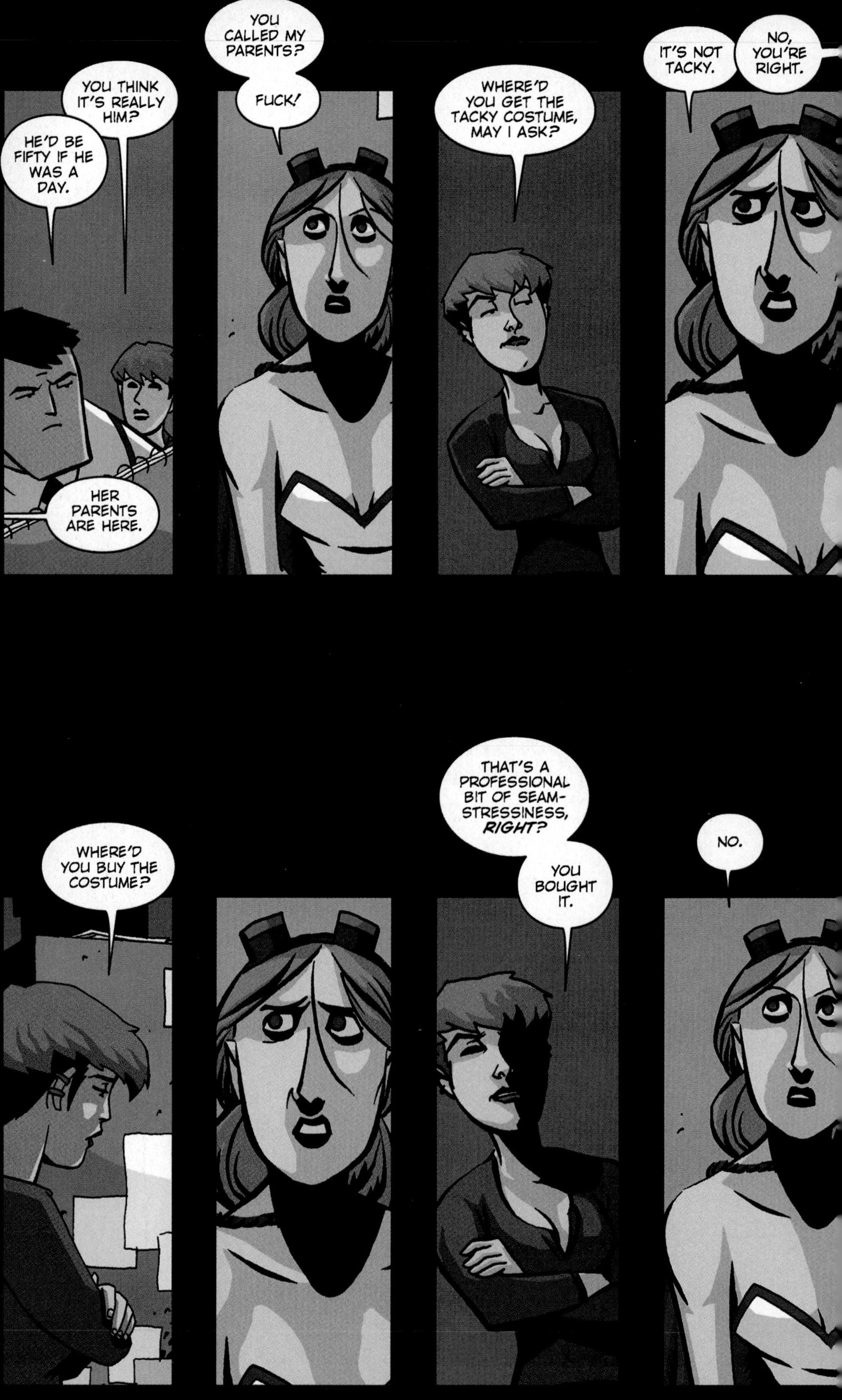
YOU THINK IT'S REALLY HIM?
HE'D BE FIFTY IF HE WAS A DAY.
HER PARENTS ARE HERE.
YOU CALLED MY PARENTS?
FUCK!
WHERE'D YOU GET THE TACKY COSTUME, MAY I ASK?
IT'S NOT TACKY.
NO, YOU'RE RIGHT.
WHERE'D YOU BUY THE COSTUME?
THAT'S A PROFESSIONAL BIT OF SEAM-STRESSINESS, *RIGHT?*
YOU BOUGHT IT.
NO.

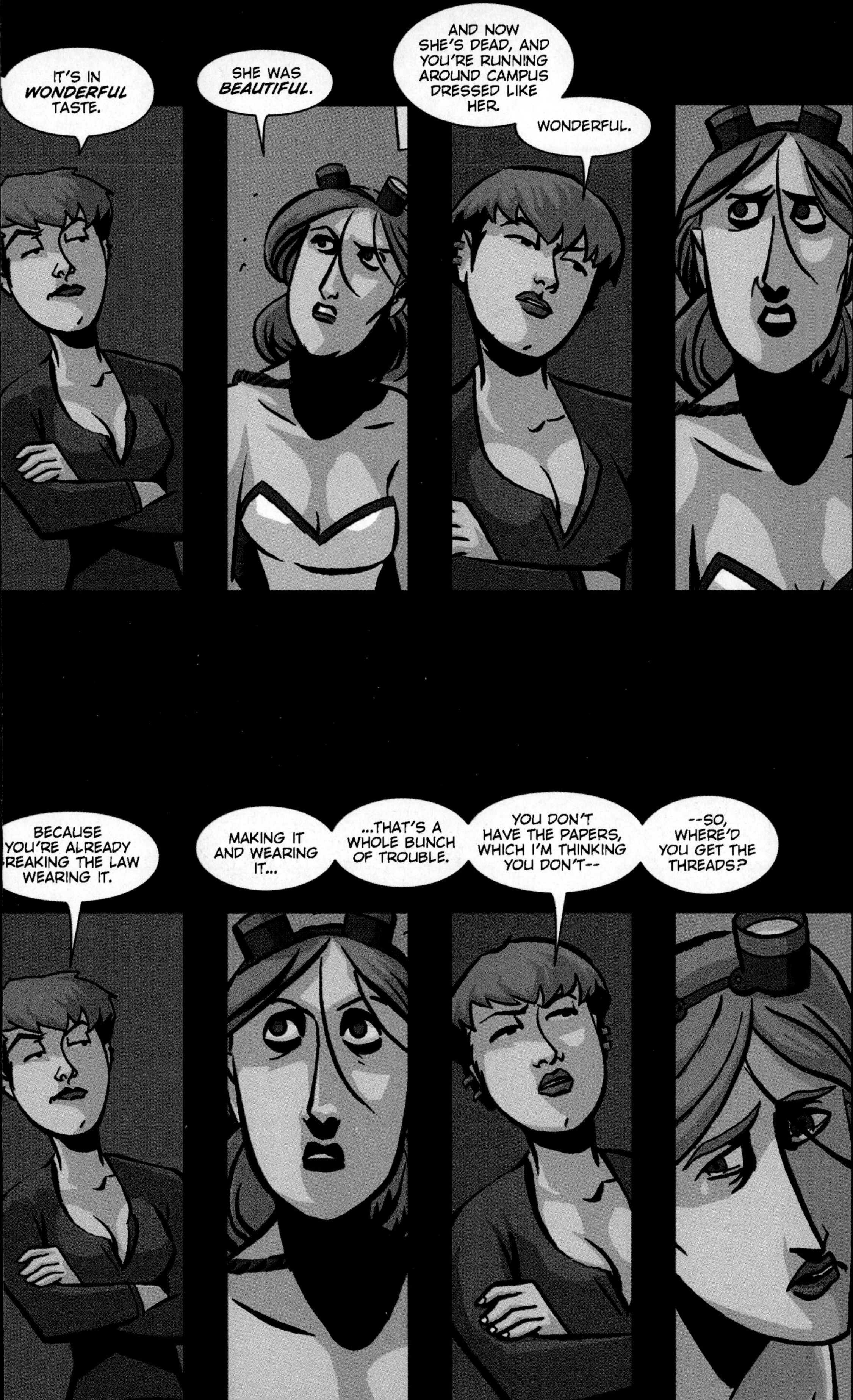
IT'S IN WONDERFUL TASTE.
SHE WAS BEAUTIFUL.
AND NOW SHE'S DEAD, AND YOU'RE RUNNING AROUND CAMPUS DRESSED LIKE HER.
WONDERFUL.
BECAUSE YOU'RE ALREADY BREAKING THE LAW WEARING IT.
MAKING IT AND WEARING IT...
...THAT'S A WHOLE BUNCH OF TROUBLE.
YOU DON'T HAVE THE PAPERS, WHICH I'M THINKING YOU DON'T--
--SO, WHERE'D YOU GET THE THREADS?

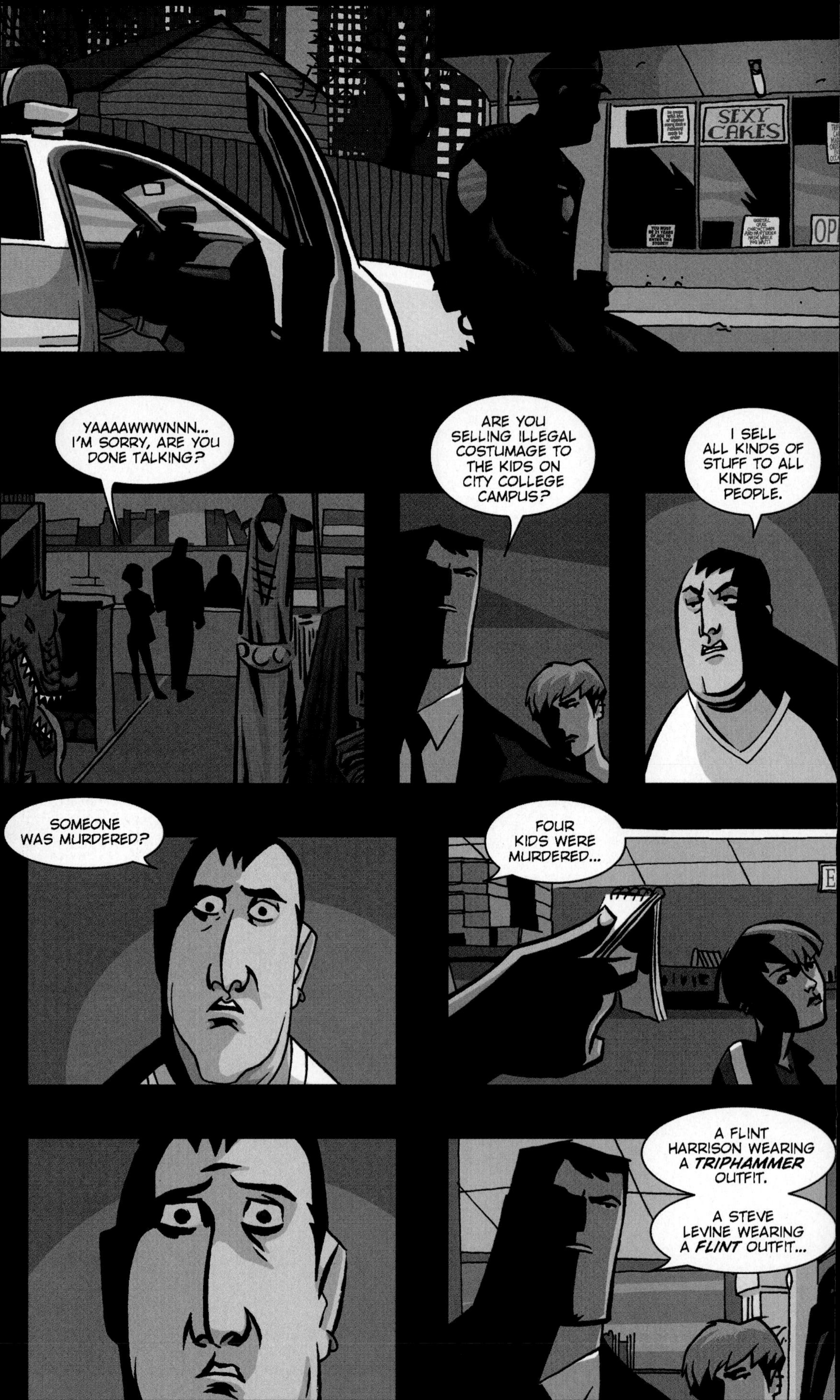
SEXY CAKES
YAAAAWWWNNN... I'M SORRY, ARE YOU DONE TALKING?
ARE YOU SELLING ILLEGAL COSTUMAGE TO THE KIDS ON CITY COLLEGE CAMPUS?
I SELL ALL KINDS OF STUFF TO ALL KINDS OF PEOPLE.
SOMEONE WAS MURDERED?
FOUR KIDS WERE MURDERED...
A FLINT HARRISON WEARING A *TRIPHAMMER* OUTFIT.
A STEVE LEVINE WEARING A *FLINT* OUTFIT...

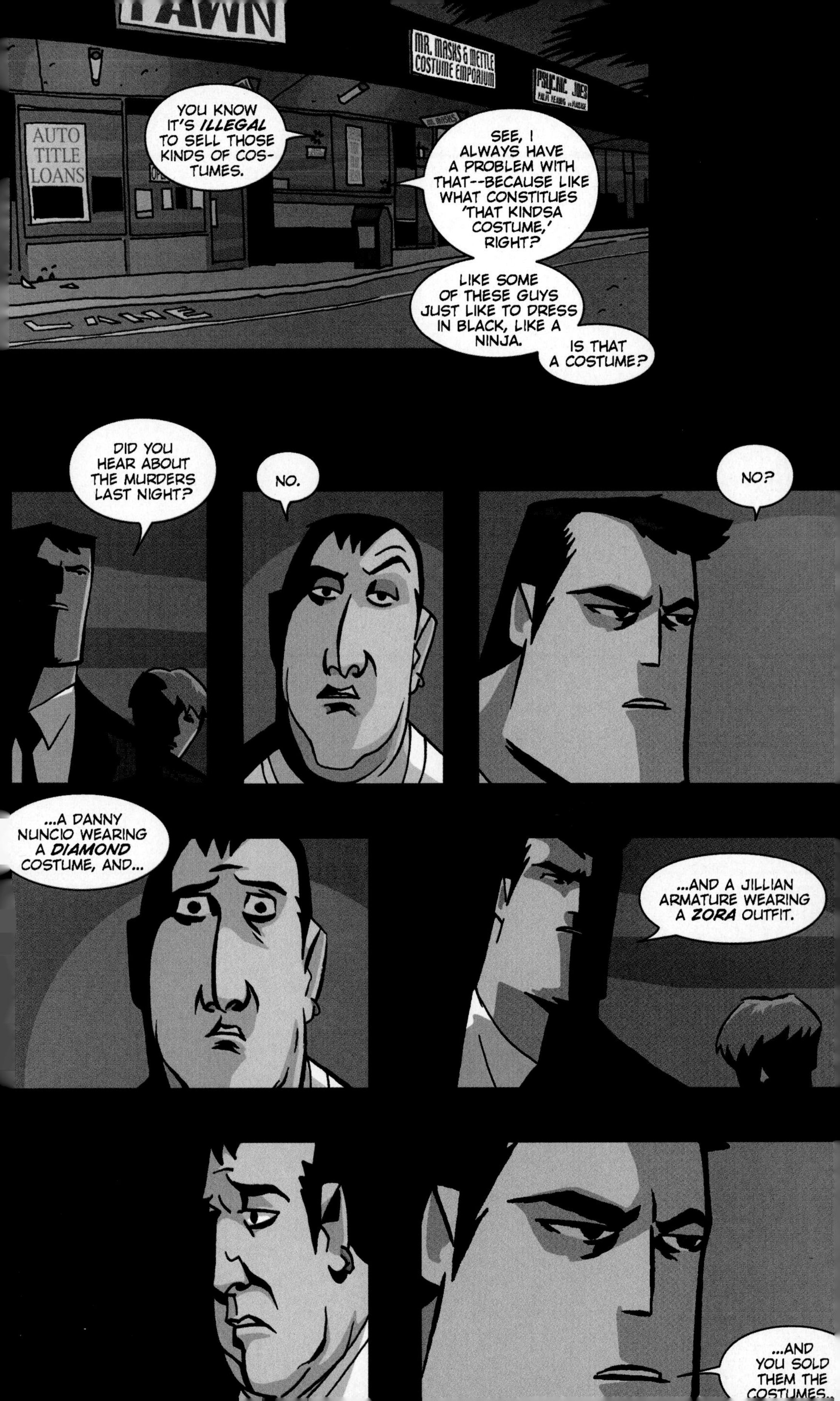
PAWN
MR. MASKS & METTLE COSTUME EMPORIUM
PSYCHIC JOES
AUTO TITLE LOANS
LANE
YOU KNOW IT'S *ILLEGAL* TO SELL THOSE KINDS OF COS-TUMES.
SEE, I ALWAYS HAVE A PROBLEM WITH THAT--BECAUSE LIKE WHAT CONSTITUES 'THAT KINDSA COSTUME,' RIGHT?
LIKE SOME OF THESE GUYS JUST LIKE TO DRESS IN BLACK, LIKE A NINJA.
IS THAT A COSTUME?
DID YOU HEAR ABOUT THE MURDERS LAST NIGHT?
NO.
NO?
...A DANNY NUNCIO WEARING A *DIAMOND* COSTUME, AND...
...AND A JILLIAN ARMATURE WEARING A *ZORA* OUTFIT.
...AND YOU SOLD THEM THE COSTUMES..

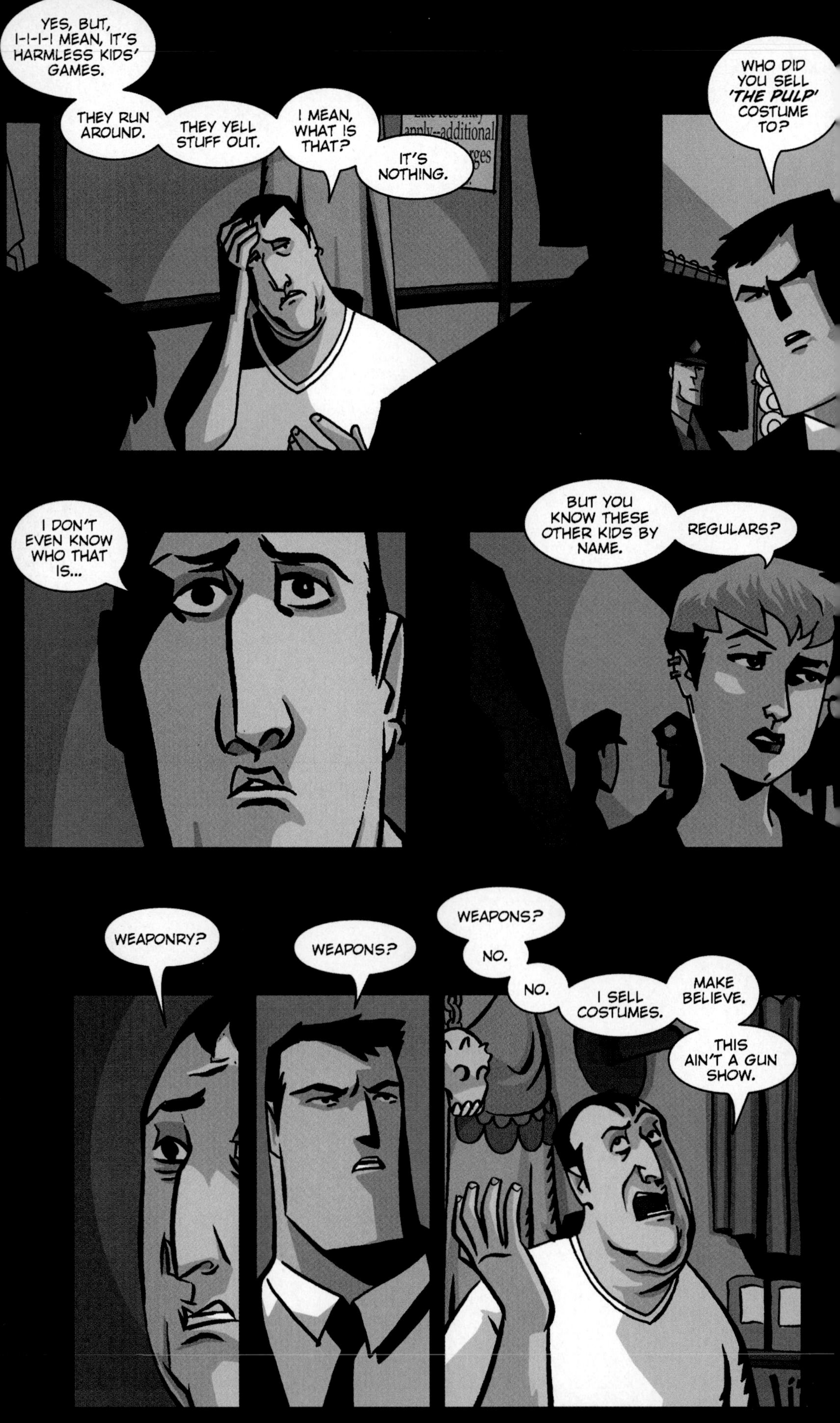
YES, BUT, I-I-I-I MEAN, IT'S HARMLESS KIDS' GAMES.
THEY RUN AROUND.
THEY YELL STUFF OUT.
I MEAN, WHAT IS THAT?
IT'S NOTHING.
WHO DID YOU SELL *'THE PULP'* COSTUME TO?
I DON'T EVEN KNOW WHO THAT IS...
BUT YOU KNOW THESE OTHER KIDS BY NAME.
REGULARS?
WEAPONRY?
WEAPONS?
WEAPONS?
NO.
NO.
I SELL COSTUMES.
MAKE BELIEVE.
THIS AIN'T A GUN SHOW.

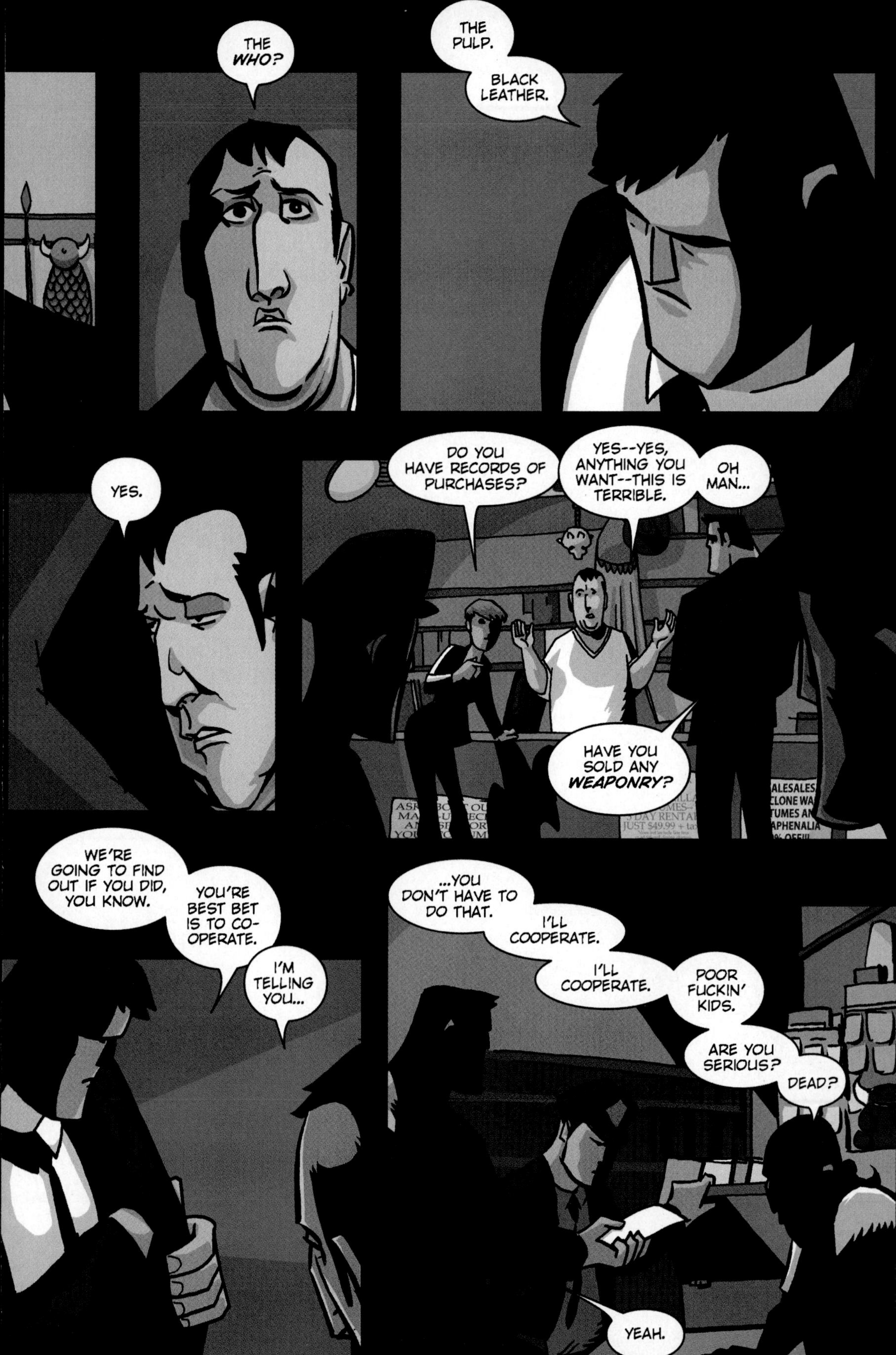
THE *WHO?*
THE PULP.
BLACK LEATHER.
YES.
DO YOU HAVE RECORDS OF PURCHASES?
YES--YES, ANYTHING YOU WANT--THIS IS TERRIBLE.
OH MAN...
HAVE YOU SOLD ANY *WEAPONRY?*
WE'RE GOING TO FIND OUT IF YOU DID, YOU KNOW.
YOU'RE BEST BET IS TO CO-OPERATE.
I'M TELLING YOU...
...YOU DON'T HAVE TO DO THAT.
I'LL COOPERATE.
I'LL COOPERATE.
POOR FUCKIN' KIDS.
ARE YOU SERIOUS?
DEAD?
YEAH.

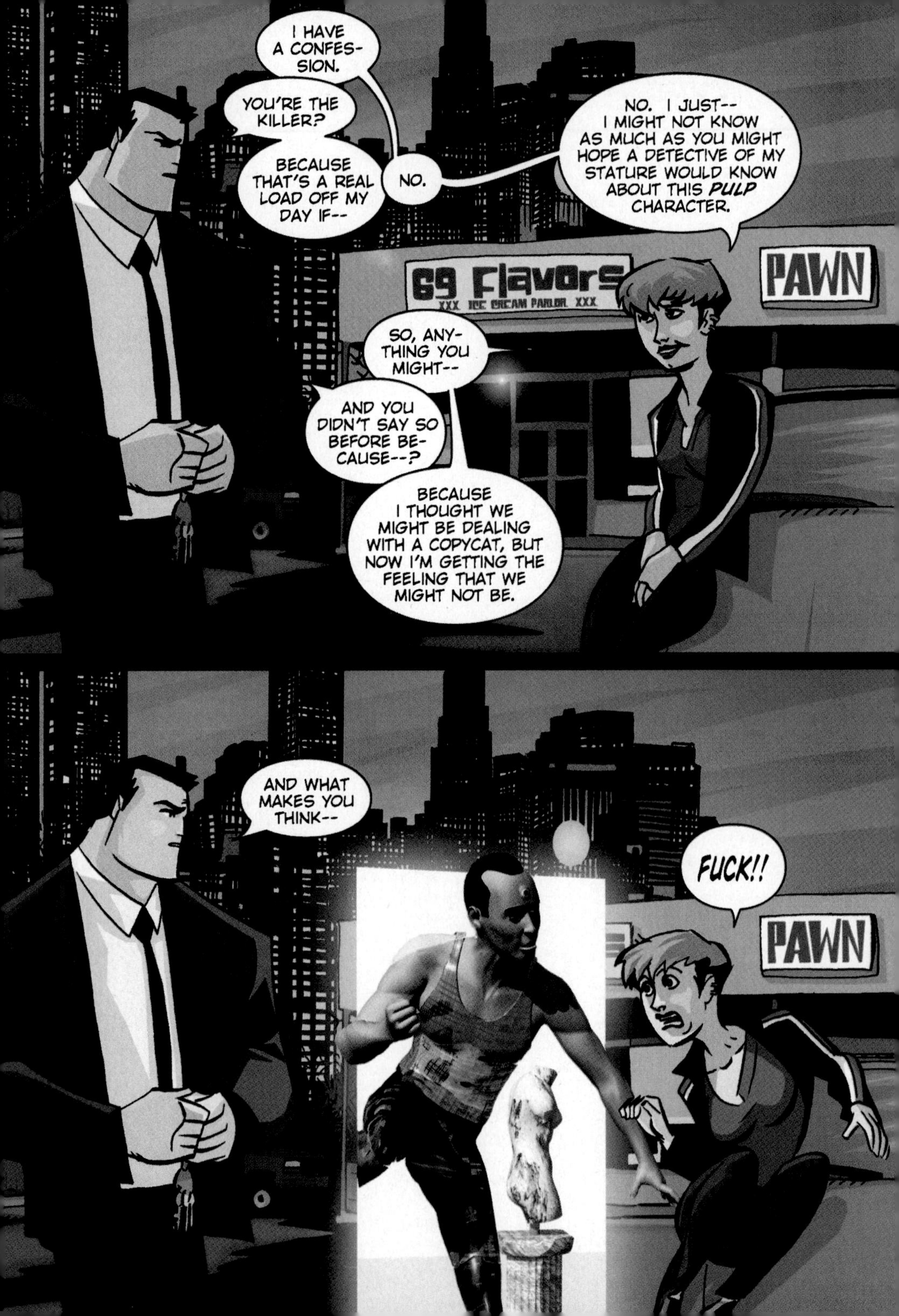
I HAVE A CONFESSION.
YOU'RE THE KILLER?
BECAUSE THAT'S A REAL LOAD OFF MY DAY IF--
NO.
NO. I JUST-- I MIGHT NOT KNOW AS MUCH AS YOU MIGHT HOPE A DETECTIVE OF MY STATURE WOULD KNOW ABOUT THIS *PULP* CHARACTER.
69 Flavors
XXX ICE CREAM PARLOR XXX
PAWN
SO, ANYTHING YOU MIGHT--
AND YOU DIDN'T SAY SO BEFORE BECAUSE--?
BECAUSE I THOUGHT WE MIGHT BE DEALING WITH A COPYCAT, BUT NOW I'M GETTING THE FEELING THAT WE MIGHT NOT BE.
AND WHAT MAKES YOU THINK--
FUCK!!
PAWN

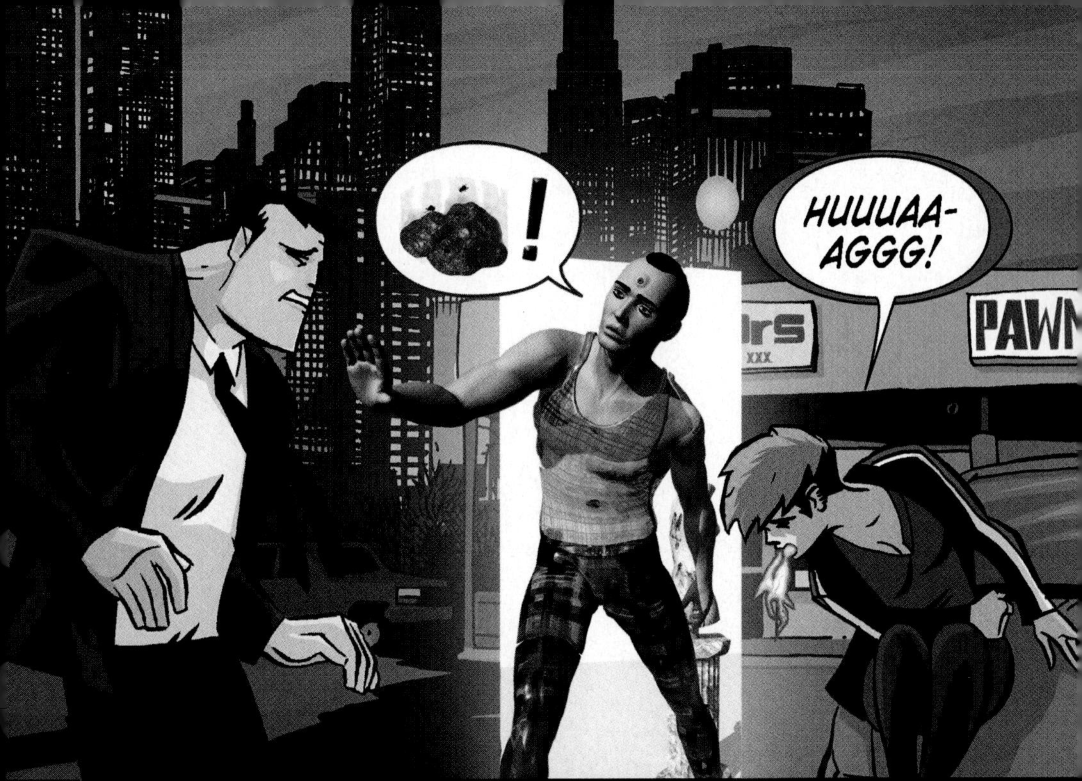
!
HUUUAA-AGGG!
PAWN
XXX

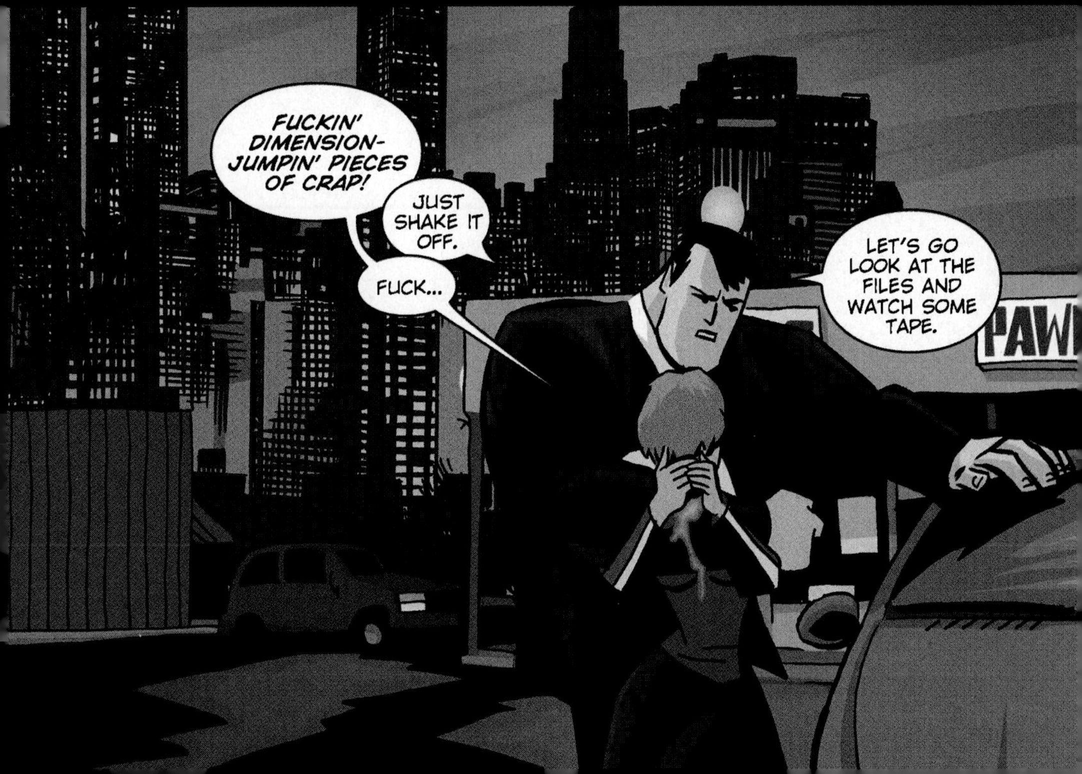
FUCKIN' DIMENSION-JUMPIN' PIECES OF CRAP!
JUST SHAKE IT OFF.
FUCK...
LET'S GO LOOK AT THE FILES AND WATCH SOME TAPE.
PAWN

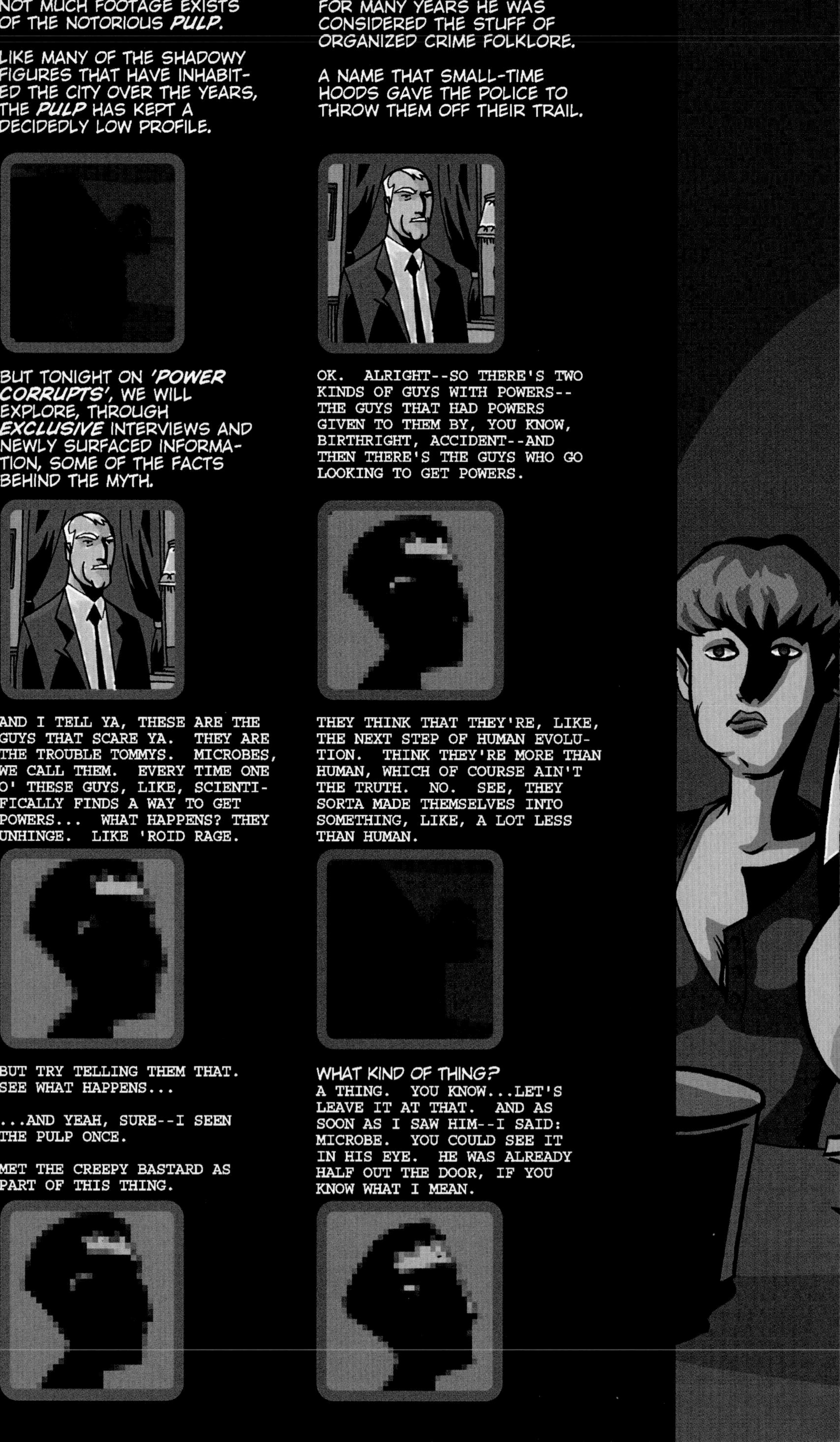
NOT MUCH FOOTAGE EXISTS OF THE NOTORIOUS *PULP.*
LIKE MANY OF THE SHADOWY FIGURES THAT HAVE INHABIT-ED THE CITY OVER THE YEARS, THE *PULP* HAS KEPT A DECIDEDLY LOW PROFILE.
FOR MANY YEARS HE WAS CONSIDERED THE STUFF OF ORGANIZED CRIME FOLKLORE.
A NAME THAT SMALL-TIME HOODS GAVE THE POLICE TO THROW THEM OFF THEIR TRAIL.
BUT TONIGHT ON *'POWER CORRUPTS'*, WE WILL EXPLORE, THROUGH *EXCLUSIVE* INTERVIEWS AND NEWLY SURFACED INFORMA-TION, SOME OF THE FACTS BEHIND THE MYTH.
OK. ALRIGHT--SO THERE'S TWO KINDS OF GUYS WITH POWERS--THE GUYS THAT HAD POWERS GIVEN TO THEM BY, YOU KNOW, BIRTHRIGHT, ACCIDENT--AND THEN THERE'S THE GUYS WHO GO LOOKING TO GET POWERS.
AND I TELL YA, THESE ARE THE GUYS THAT SCARE YA. THEY ARE THE TROUBLE TOMMYS. MICROBES, WE CALL THEM. EVERY TIME ONE O' THESE GUYS, LIKE, SCIENTI-FICALLY FINDS A WAY TO GET POWERS... WHAT HAPPENS? THEY UNHINGE. LIKE 'ROID RAGE.
THEY THINK THAT THEY'RE, LIKE, THE NEXT STEP OF HUMAN EVOLU-TION. THINK THEY'RE MORE THAN HUMAN, WHICH OF COURSE AIN'T THE TRUTH. NO. SEE, THEY SORTA MADE THEMSELVES INTO SOMETHING, LIKE, A LOT LESS THAN HUMAN.
BUT TRY TELLING THEM THAT. SEE WHAT HAPPENS...
...AND YEAH, SURE--I SEEN THE PULP ONCE.
MET THE CREEPY BASTARD AS PART OF THIS THING.
WHAT KIND OF THING?
A THING. YOU KNOW...LET'S LEAVE IT AT THAT. AND AS SOON AS I SAW HIM--I SAID: MICROBE. YOU COULD SEE IT IN HIS EYE. HE WAS ALREADY HALF OUT THE DOOR, IF YOU KNOW WHAT I MEAN.

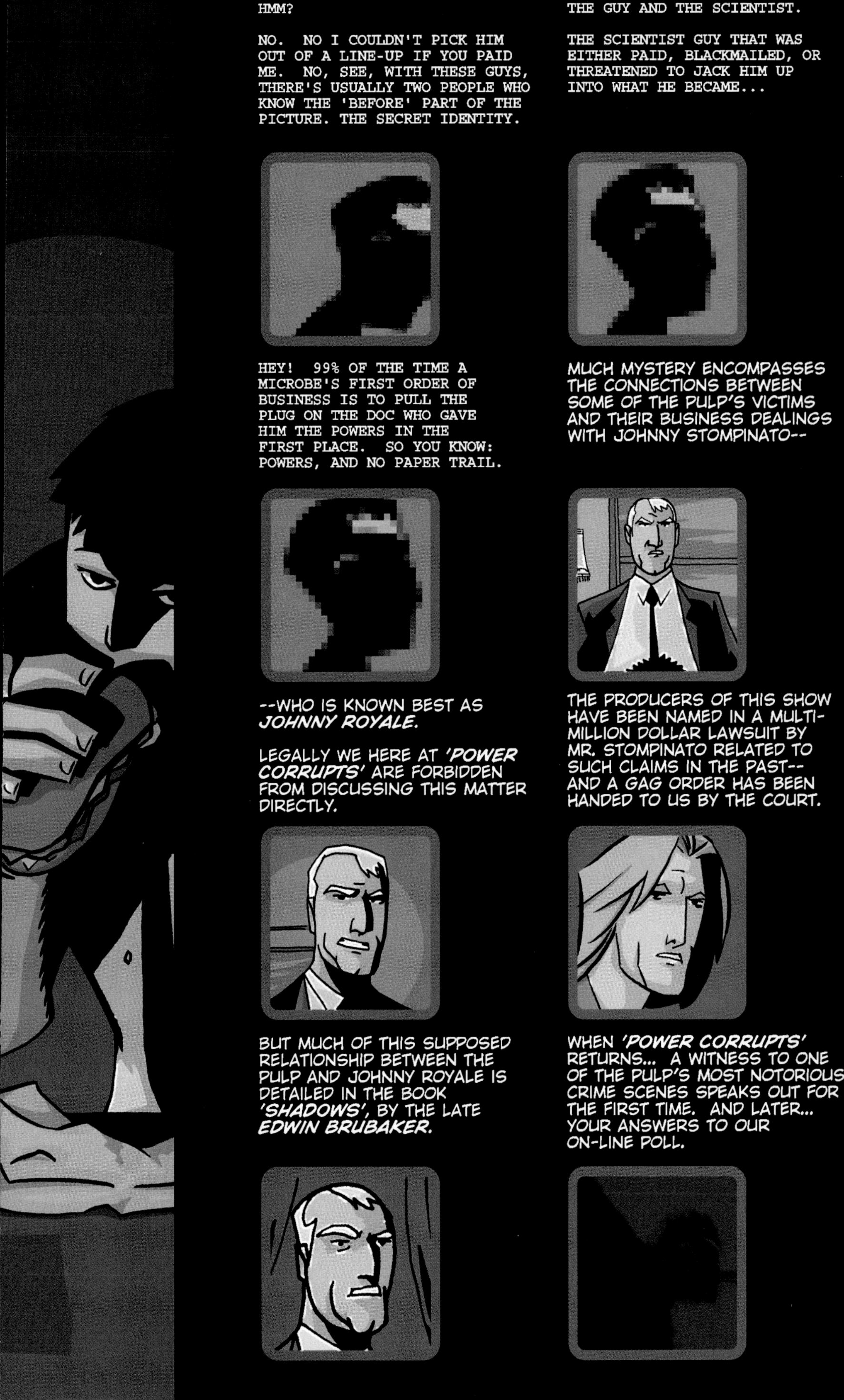

HMM?
NO. NO I COULDN'T PICK HIM OUT OF A LINE-UP IF YOU PAID ME. NO, SEE, WITH THESE GUYS, THERE'S USUALLY TWO PEOPLE WHO KNOW THE 'BEFORE' PART OF THE PICTURE. THE SECRET IDENTITY.
THE GUY AND THE SCIENTIST.
THE SCIENTIST GUY THAT WAS EITHER PAID, BLACKMAILED, OR THREATENED TO JACK HIM UP INTO WHAT HE BECAME...
HEY! 99% OF THE TIME A MICROBE'S FIRST ORDER OF BUSINESS IS TO PULL THE PLUG ON THE DOC WHO GAVE HIM THE POWERS IN THE FIRST PLACE. SO YOU KNOW: POWERS, AND NO PAPER TRAIL.
MUCH MYSTERY ENCOMPASSES THE CONNECTIONS BETWEEN SOME OF THE PULP'S VICTIMS AND THEIR BUSINESS DEALINGS WITH JOHNNY STOMPINATO--
--WHO IS KNOWN BEST AS *JOHNNY ROYALE.*
LEGALLY WE HERE AT *'POWER CORRUPTS'* ARE FORBIDDEN FROM DISCUSSING THIS MATTER DIRECTLY.
THE PRODUCERS OF THIS SHOW HAVE BEEN NAMED IN A MULTI-MILLION DOLLAR LAWSUIT BY MR. STOMPINATO RELATED TO SUCH CLAIMS IN THE PAST-- AND A GAG ORDER HAS BEEN HANDED TO US BY THE COURT.
BUT MUCH OF THIS SUPPOSED RELATIONSHIP BETWEEN THE PULP AND JOHNNY ROYALE IS DETAILED IN THE BOOK *'SHADOWS'*, BY THE LATE *EDWIN BRUBAKER.*
WHEN *'POWER CORRUPTS'* RETURNS... A WITNESS TO ONE OF THE PULP'S MOST NOTORIOUS CRIME SCENES SPEAKS OUT FOR THE FIRST TIME. AND LATER... YOUR ANSWERS TO OUR ON-LINE POLL.

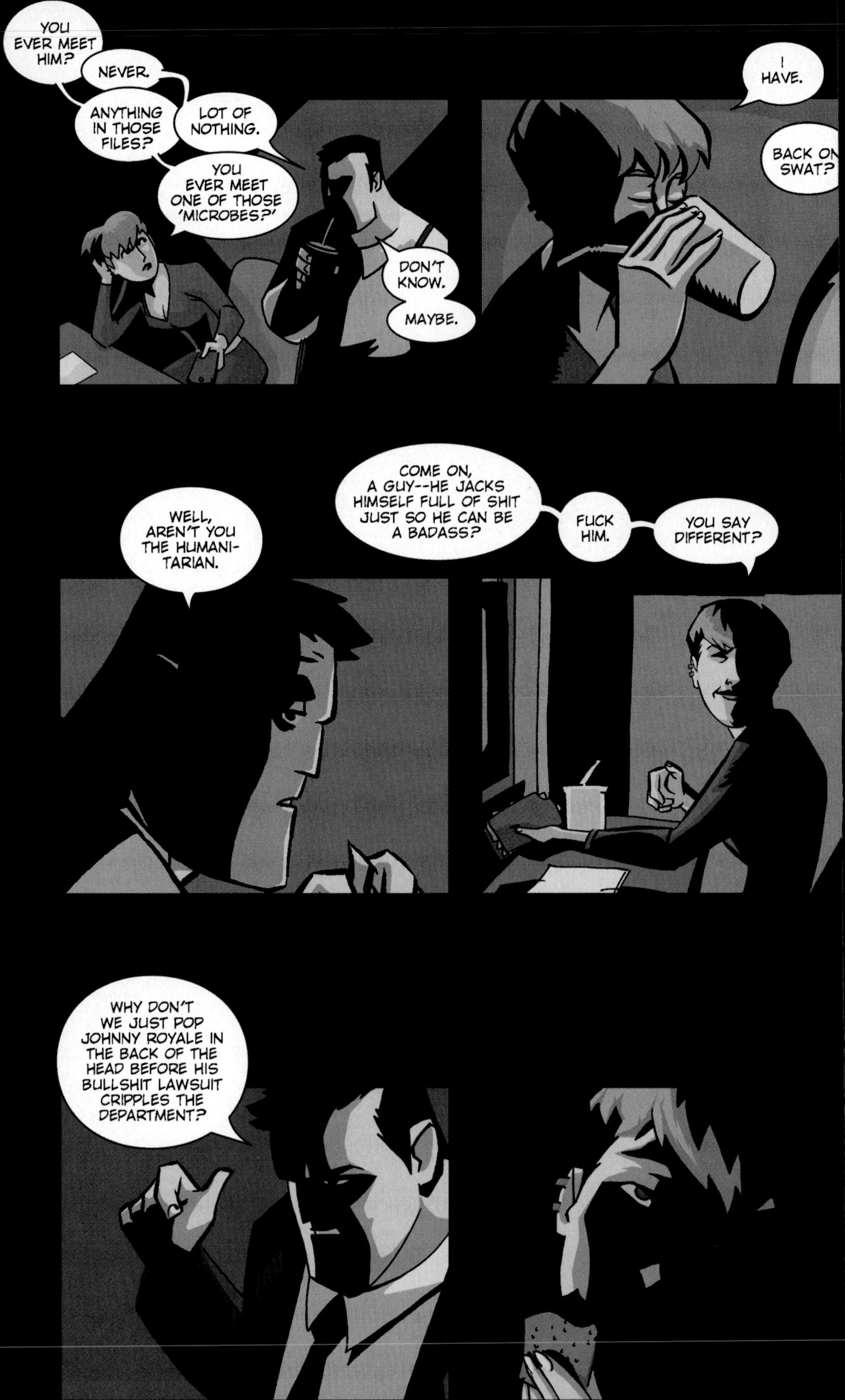
YOU EVER MEET HIM?
NEVER.
ANYTHING IN THOSE FILES?
LOT OF NOTHING.
YOU EVER MEET ONE OF THOSE 'MICROBES?'
DON'T KNOW.
MAYBE.
I HAVE.
BACK ON SWAT?
COME ON, A GUY--HE JACKS HIMSELF FULL OF SHIT JUST SO HE CAN BE A BADASS?
FUCK HIM.
YOU SAY DIFFERENT?
WELL, AREN'T YOU THE HUMANITARIAN.
WHY DON'T WE JUST POP JOHNNY ROYALE IN THE BACK OF THE HEAD BEFORE HIS BULLSHIT LAWSUIT CRIPPLES THE DEPARTMENT?

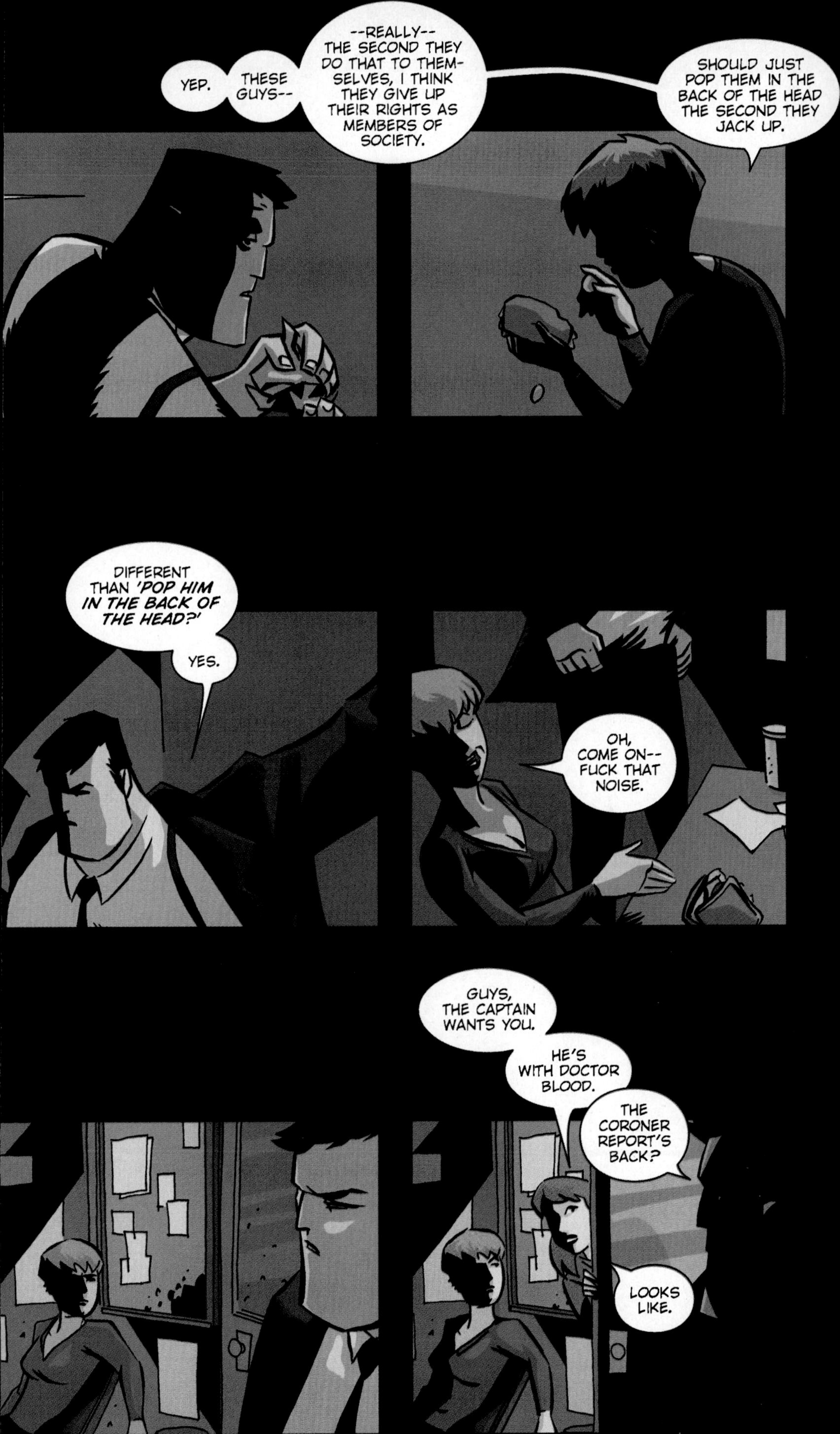
YEP.
THESE GUYS--
--REALLY-- THE SECOND THEY DO THAT TO THEM-SELVES, I THINK THEY GIVE UP THEIR RIGHTS AS MEMBERS OF SOCIETY.
SHOULD JUST POP THEM IN THE BACK OF THE HEAD THE SECOND THEY JACK UP.
DIFFERENT THAN *'POP HIM IN THE BACK OF THE HEAD?'*
YES.
OH, COME ON-- FUCK THAT NOISE.
GUYS, THE CAPTAIN WANTS YOU.
HE'S WITH DOCTOR BLOOD.
THE CORONER REPORT'S BACK?
LOOKS LIKE.

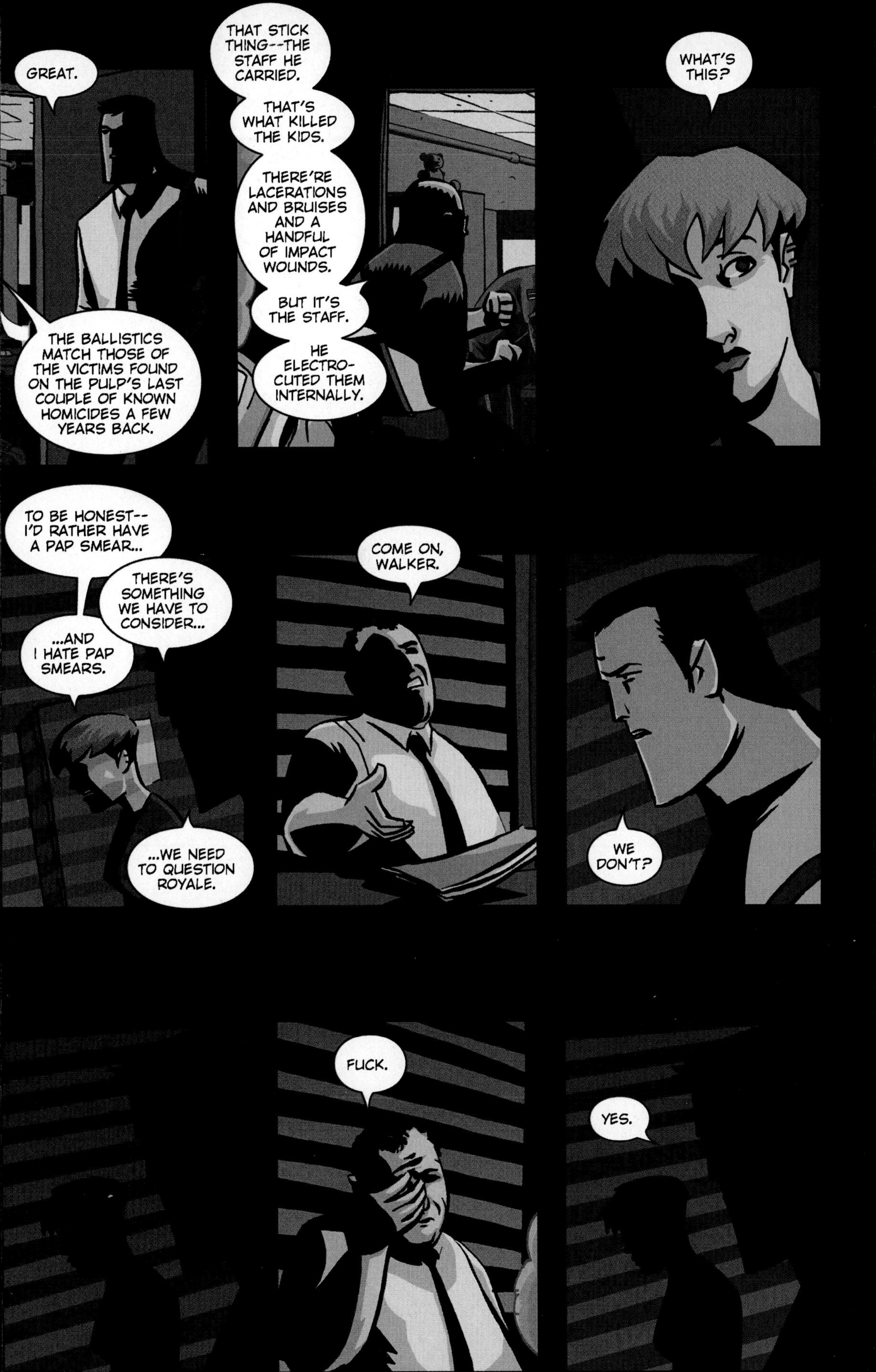
GREAT.
THE BALLISTICS MATCH THOSE OF THE VICTIMS FOUND ON THE PULP'S LAST COUPLE OF KNOWN HOMICIDES A FEW YEARS BACK.
THAT STICK THING--THE STAFF HE CARRIED.
THAT'S WHAT KILLED THE KIDS.
THERE'RE LACERATIONS AND BRUISES AND A HANDFUL OF IMPACT WOUNDS.
BUT IT'S THE STAFF.
HE ELECTROCUTED THEM INTERNALLY.
WHAT'S THIS?
TO BE HONEST--I'D RATHER HAVE A PAP SMEAR...
...AND I HATE PAP SMEARS.
THERE'S SOMETHING WE HAVE TO CONSIDER...
...WE NEED TO QUESTION ROYALE.
COME ON, WALKER.
WE DON'T?
FUCK.
YES.

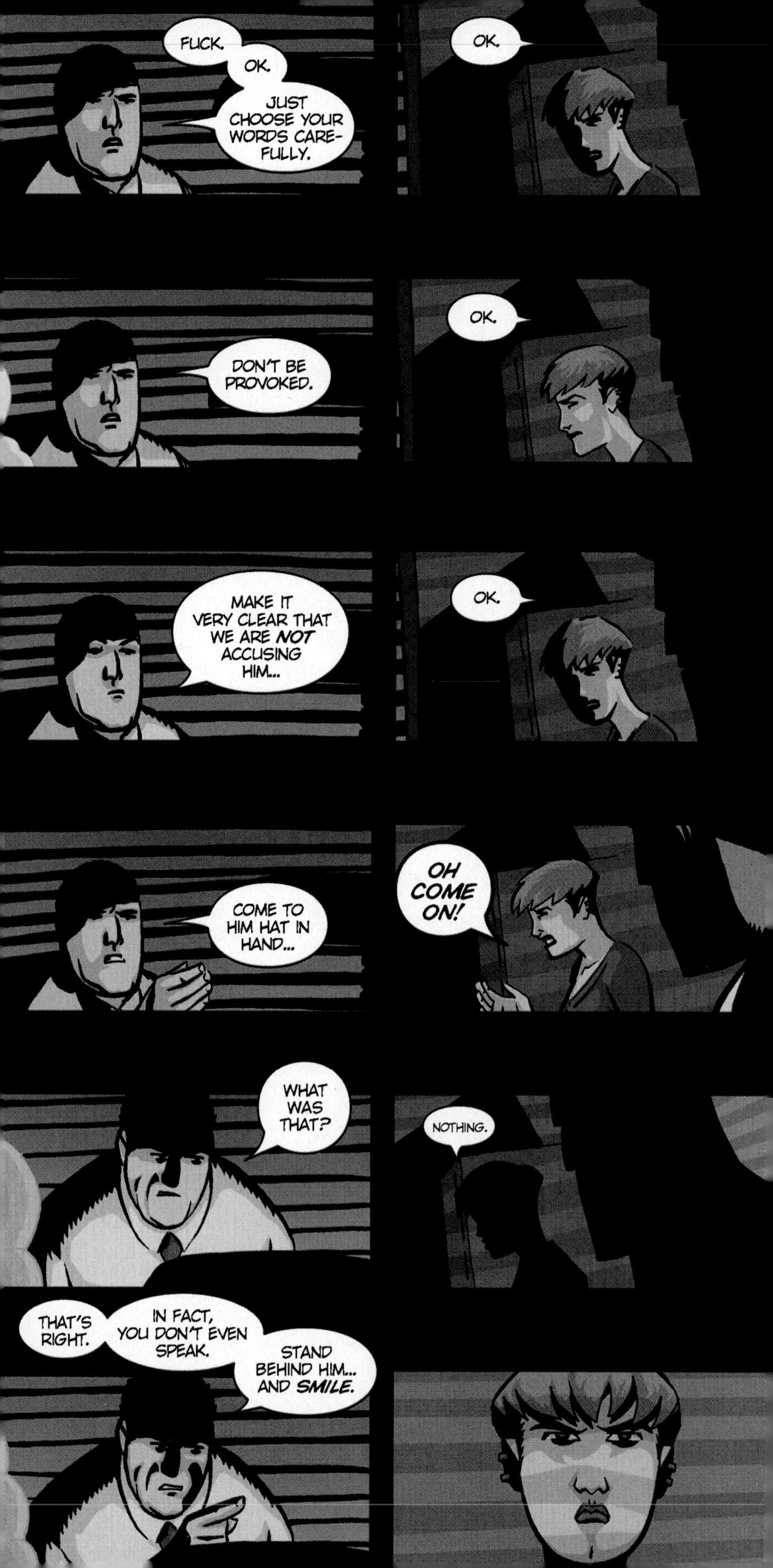
FUCK.
OK.
JUST CHOOSE YOUR WORDS CAREFULLY.
OK.
DON'T BE PROVOKED.
OK.
MAKE IT VERY CLEAR THAT WE ARE ***NOT*** ACCUSING HIM...
OK.
COME TO HIM HAT IN HAND...
OH COME ON!
WHAT WAS THAT?
NOTHING.
THAT'S RIGHT.
IN FACT, YOU DON'T EVEN SPEAK.
STAND BEHIND HIM... AND ***SMILE.***

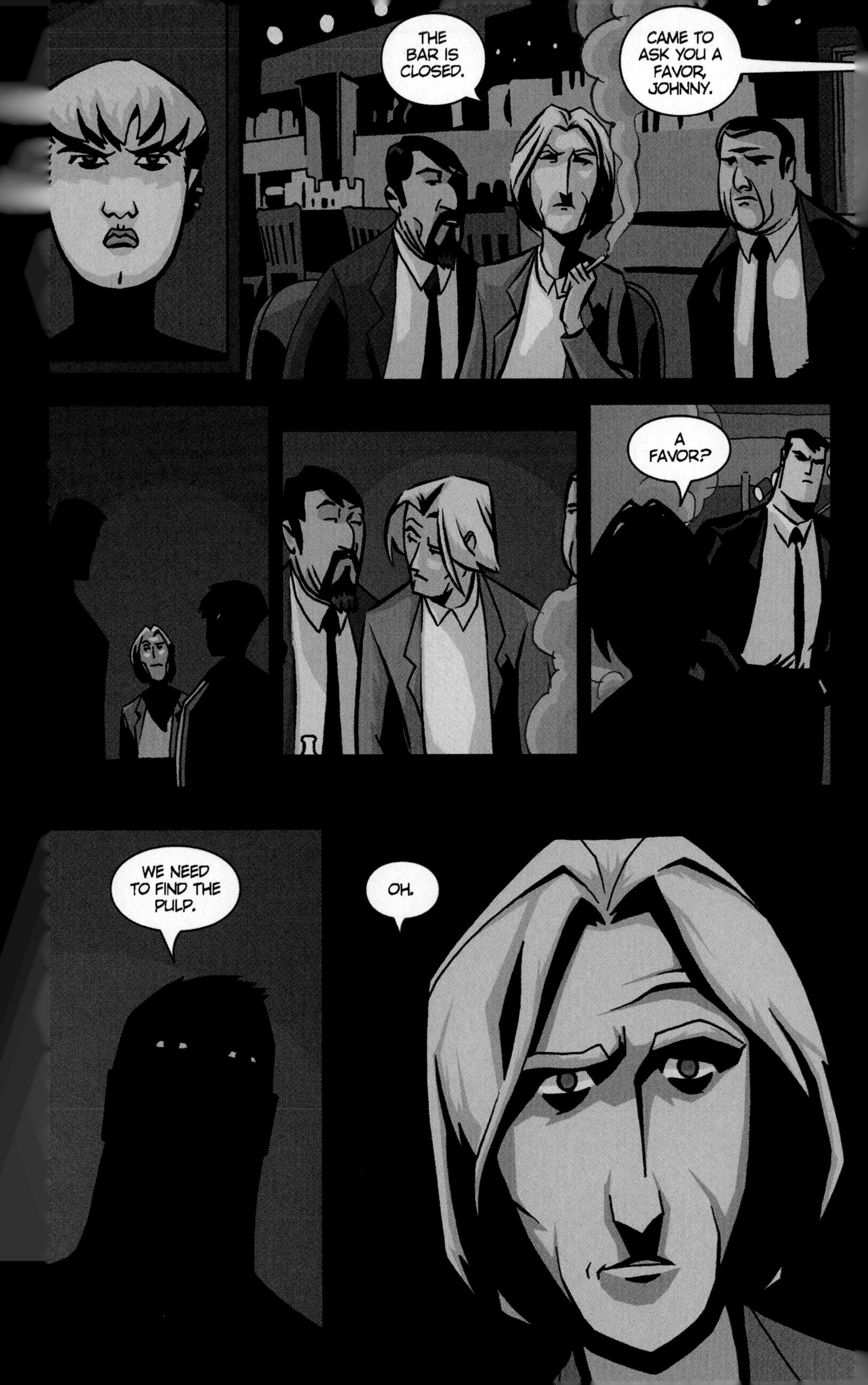
THE BAR IS CLOSED.
CAME TO ASK YOU A FAVOR, JOHNNY.
A FAVOR?
WE NEED TO FIND THE PULP.
OH.

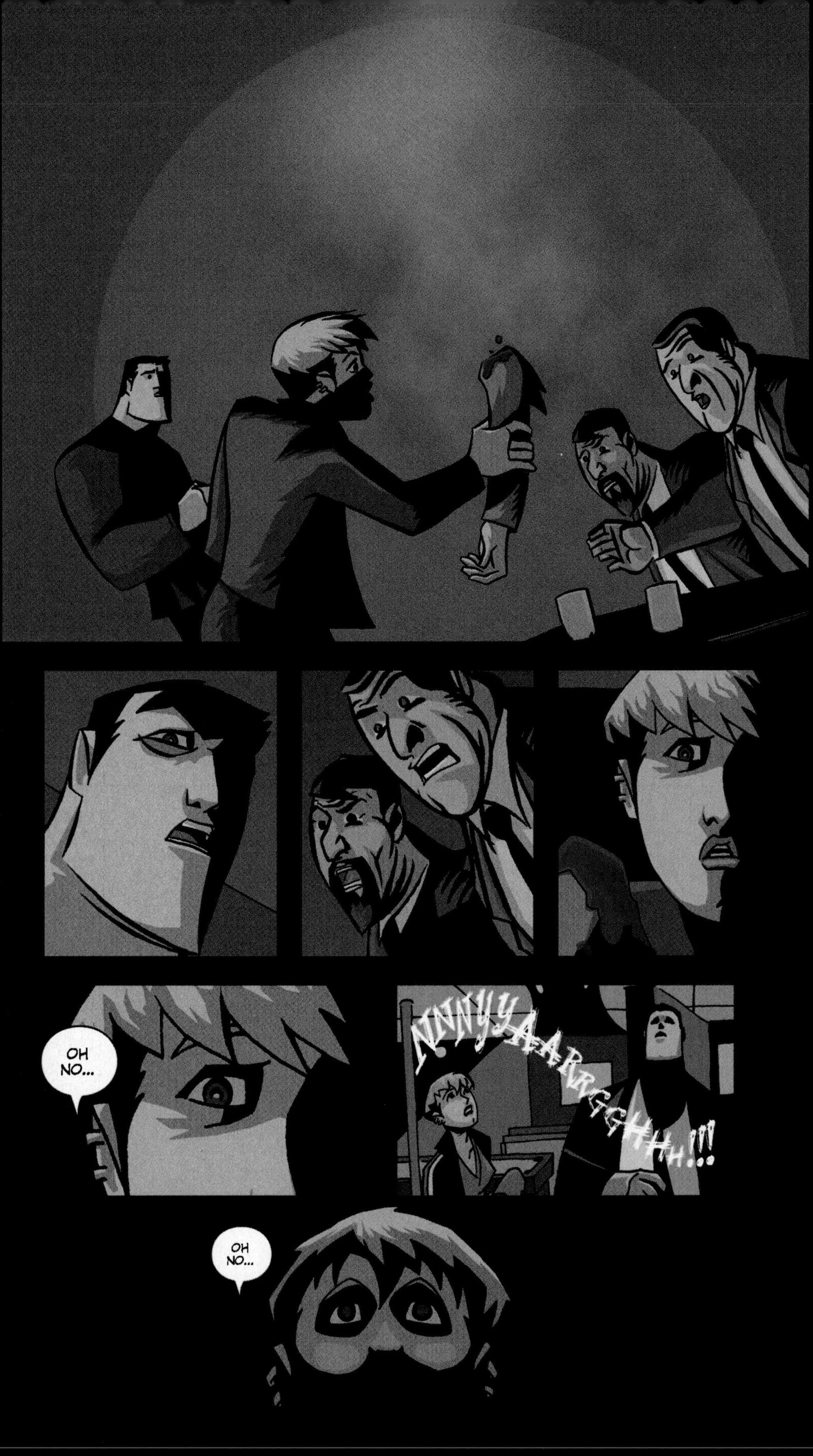
OH NO...
NINNYYAARRGGHHH!!!
OH NO...

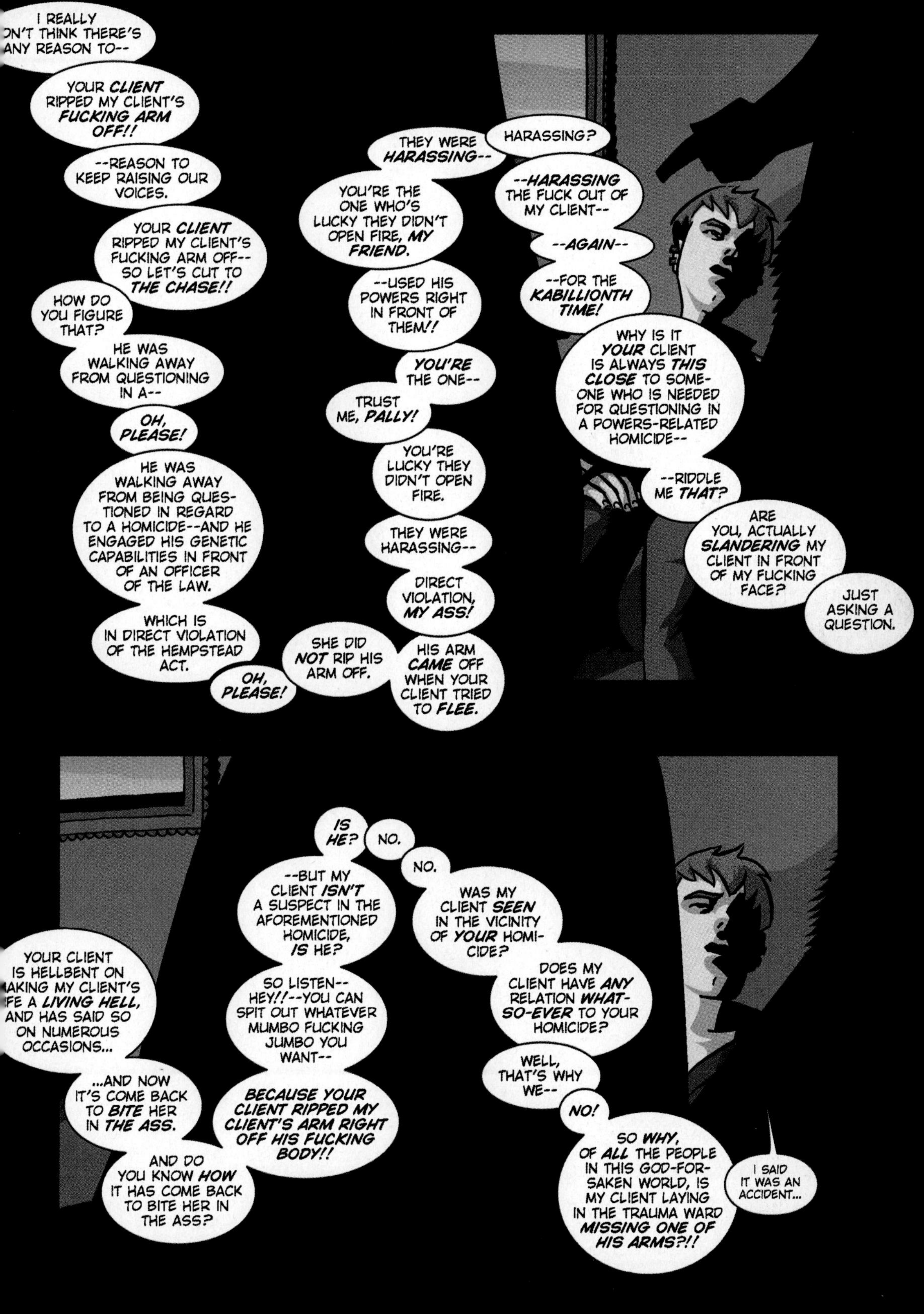
I REALLY ON'T THINK THERE'S ANY REASON TO--
YOUR *CLIENT* RIPPED MY CLIENT'S *FUCKING ARM OFF!!*
--REASON TO KEEP RAISING OUR VOICES.
YOUR *CLIENT* RIPPED MY CLIENT'S FUCKING ARM OFF-- SO LET'S CUT TO *THE CHASE!!*
HOW DO YOU FIGURE THAT?
HE WAS WALKING AWAY FROM QUESTIONING IN A--
OH, PLEASE!
HE WAS WALKING AWAY FROM BEING QUESTIONED IN REGARD TO A HOMICIDE--AND HE ENGAGED HIS GENETIC CAPABILITIES IN FRONT OF AN OFFICER OF THE LAW.
WHICH IS IN DIRECT VIOLATION OF THE HEMPSTEAD ACT.
OH, PLEASE!
THEY WERE *HARASSING--*
HARASSING?
YOU'RE THE ONE WHO'S LUCKY THEY DIDN'T OPEN FIRE, *MY FRIEND.*
--HARASSING THE FUCK OUT OF MY CLIENT--
--AGAIN--
--FOR THE *KABILLIONTH TIME!*
--USED HIS POWERS RIGHT IN FRONT OF THEM*!!*
YOU'RE THE ONE--
TRUST ME, *PALLY!*
YOU'RE LUCKY THEY DIDN'T OPEN FIRE.
THEY WERE HARASSING--
DIRECT VIOLATION, *MY ASS!*
SHE DID *NOT* RIP HIS ARM OFF.
HIS ARM *CAME* OFF WHEN YOUR CLIENT TRIED TO *FLEE.*
WHY IS IT *YOUR* CLIENT IS ALWAYS *THIS CLOSE* TO SOMEONE WHO IS NEEDED FOR QUESTIONING IN A POWERS-RELATED HOMICIDE--
--RIDDLE ME *THAT?*
ARE YOU, ACTUALLY *SLANDERING* MY CLIENT IN FRONT OF MY FUCKING FACE?
JUST ASKING A QUESTION.
YOUR CLIENT IS HELLBENT ON AKING MY CLIENT'S FE A *LIVING HELL,* AND HAS SAID SO ON NUMEROUS OCCASIONS...
...AND NOW IT'S COME BACK TO *BITE* HER IN *THE ASS.*
AND DO YOU KNOW *HOW* IT HAS COME BACK TO BITE HER IN THE ASS?
IS HE?
NO.
NO.
--BUT MY CLIENT *ISN'T* A SUSPECT IN THE AFOREMENTIONED HOMICIDE, *IS* HE?
SO LISTEN-- HEY*!!*--YOU CAN SPIT OUT WHATEVER MUMBO FUCKING JUMBO YOU WANT--
BECAUSE YOUR CLIENT RIPPED MY CLIENT'S ARM RIGHT OFF HIS FUCKING BODY!!
WAS MY CLIENT *SEEN* IN THE VICINITY OF *YOUR* HOMICIDE?
DOES MY CLIENT HAVE *ANY* RELATION *WHATSO-EVER* TO YOUR HOMICIDE?
WELL, THAT'S WHY WE--
NO!
SO *WHY,* OF *ALL* THE PEOPLE IN THIS GOD-FORSAKEN WORLD, IS MY CLIENT LAYING IN THE TRAUMA WARD *MISSING ONE OF HIS ARMS?!!*
I SAID IT WAS AN ACCIDENT...

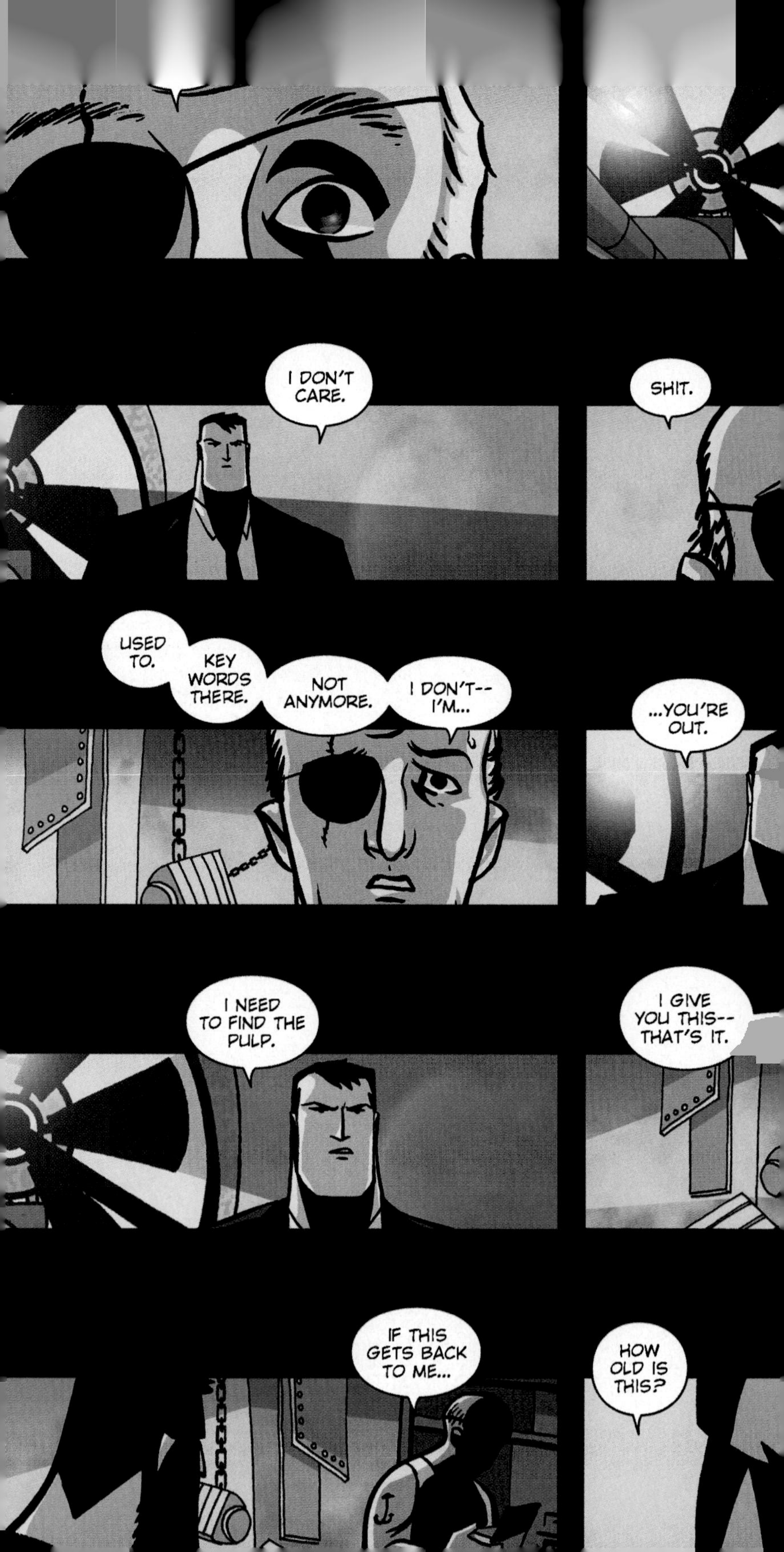

I DON'T CARE.
SHIT.
USED TO.
KEY WORDS THERE.
NOT ANYMORE.
I DON'T-- I'M...
...YOU'RE OUT.
I NEED TO FIND THE PULP.
I GIVE YOU THIS-- THAT'S IT.
IF THIS GETS BACK TO ME...
HOW OLD IS THIS?

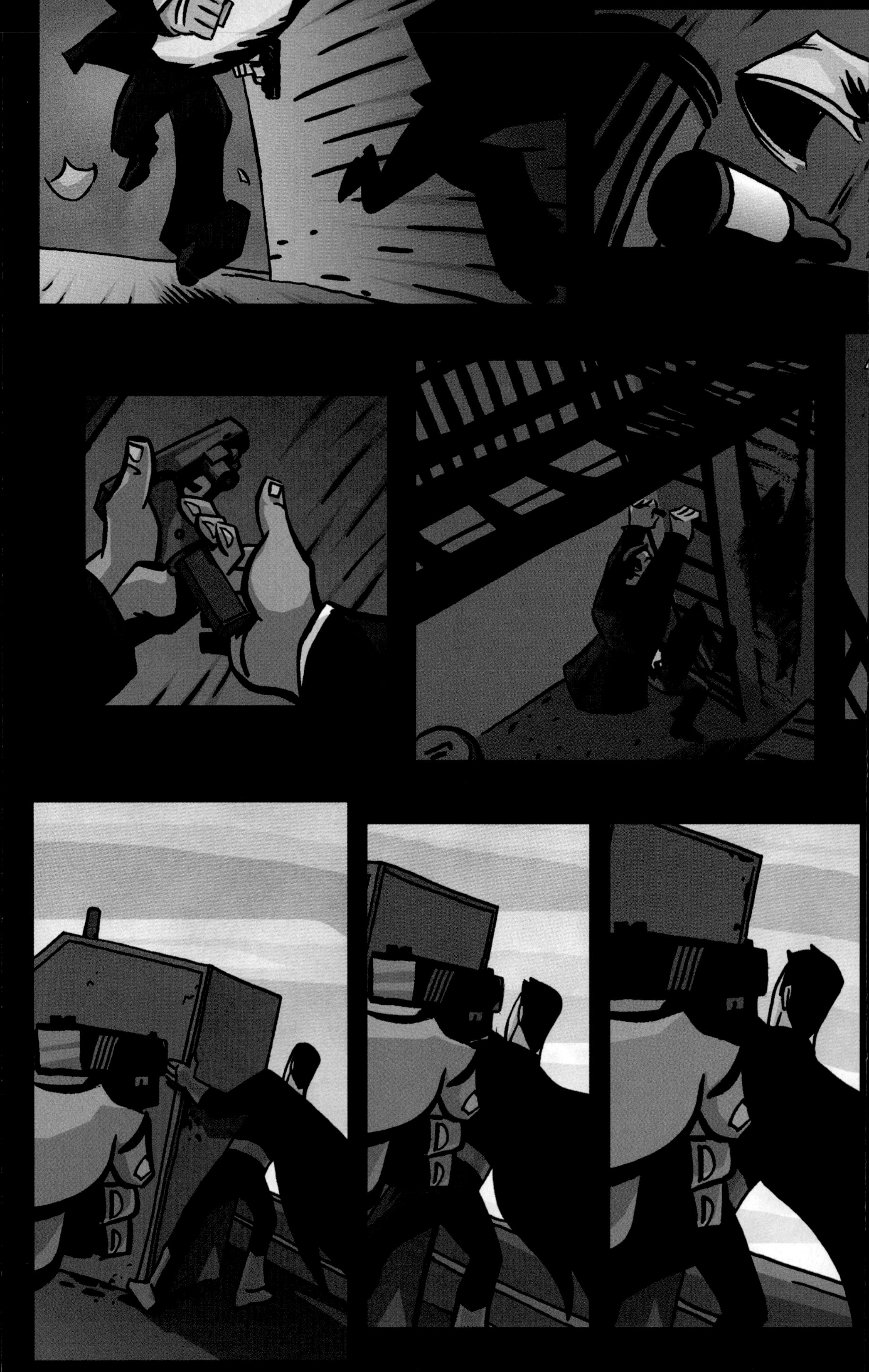

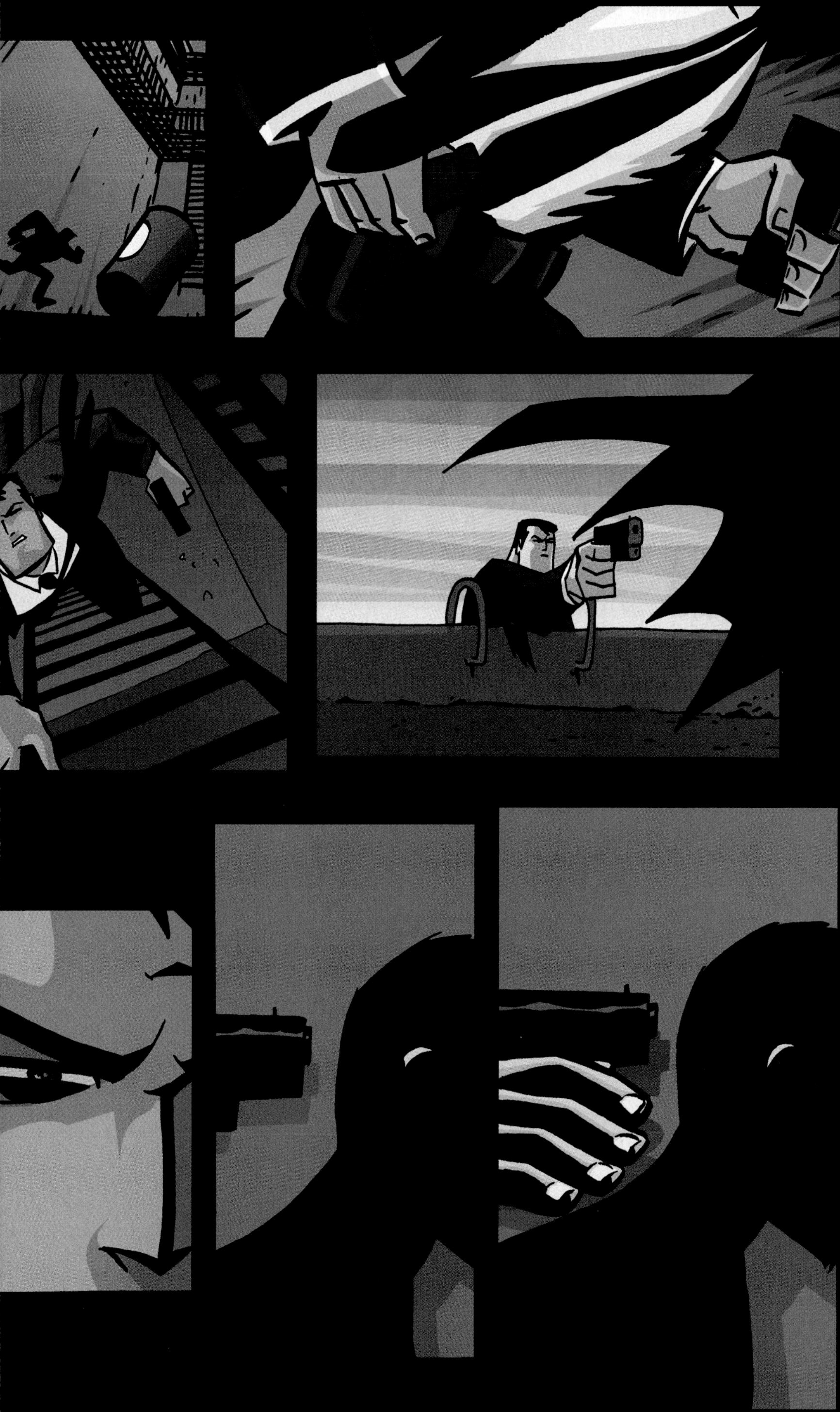

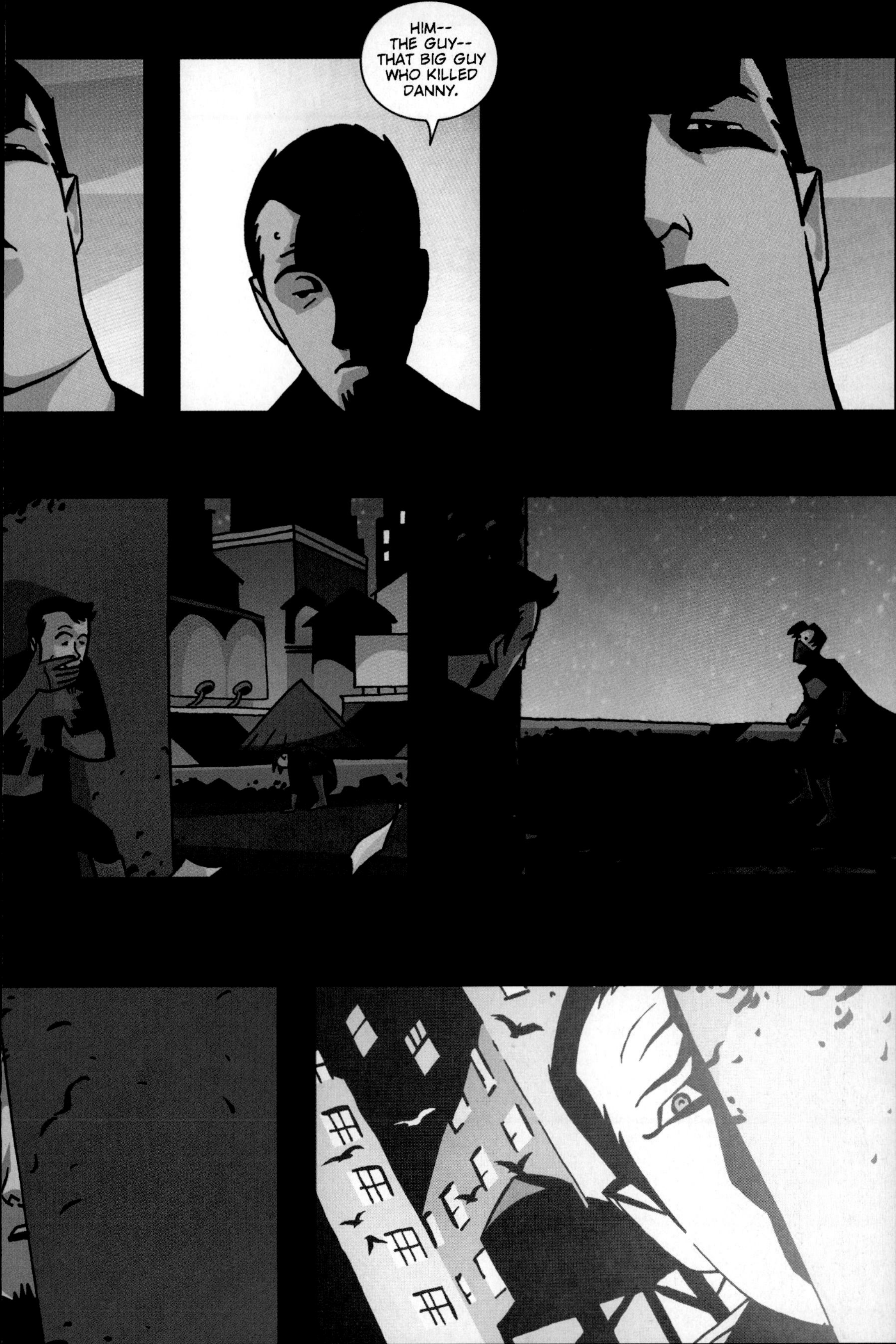
HIM-- THE GUY-- THAT BIG GUY WHO KILLED DANNY.

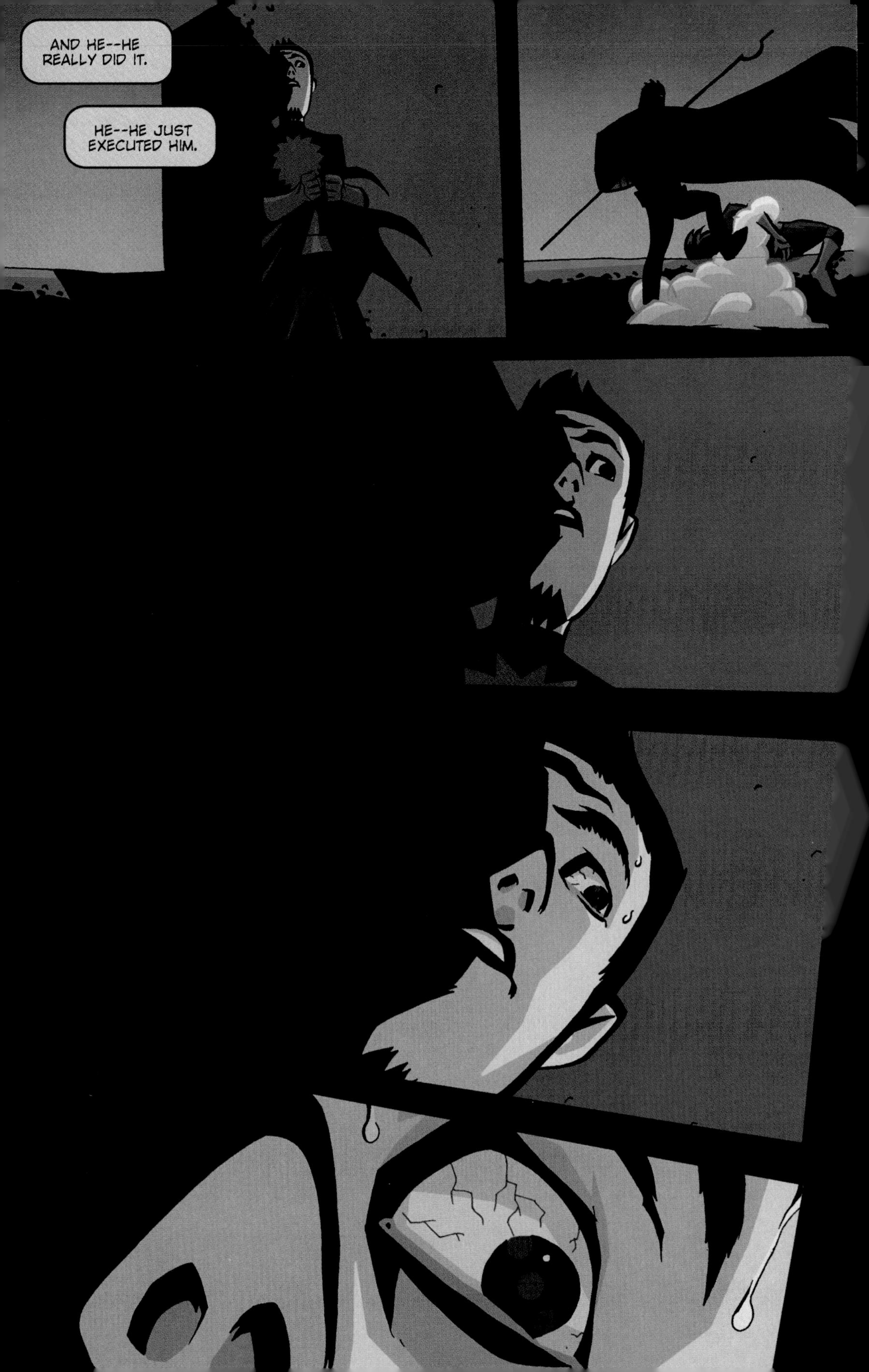
AND HE--HE REALLY DID IT.
HE--HE JUST EXECUTED HIM.

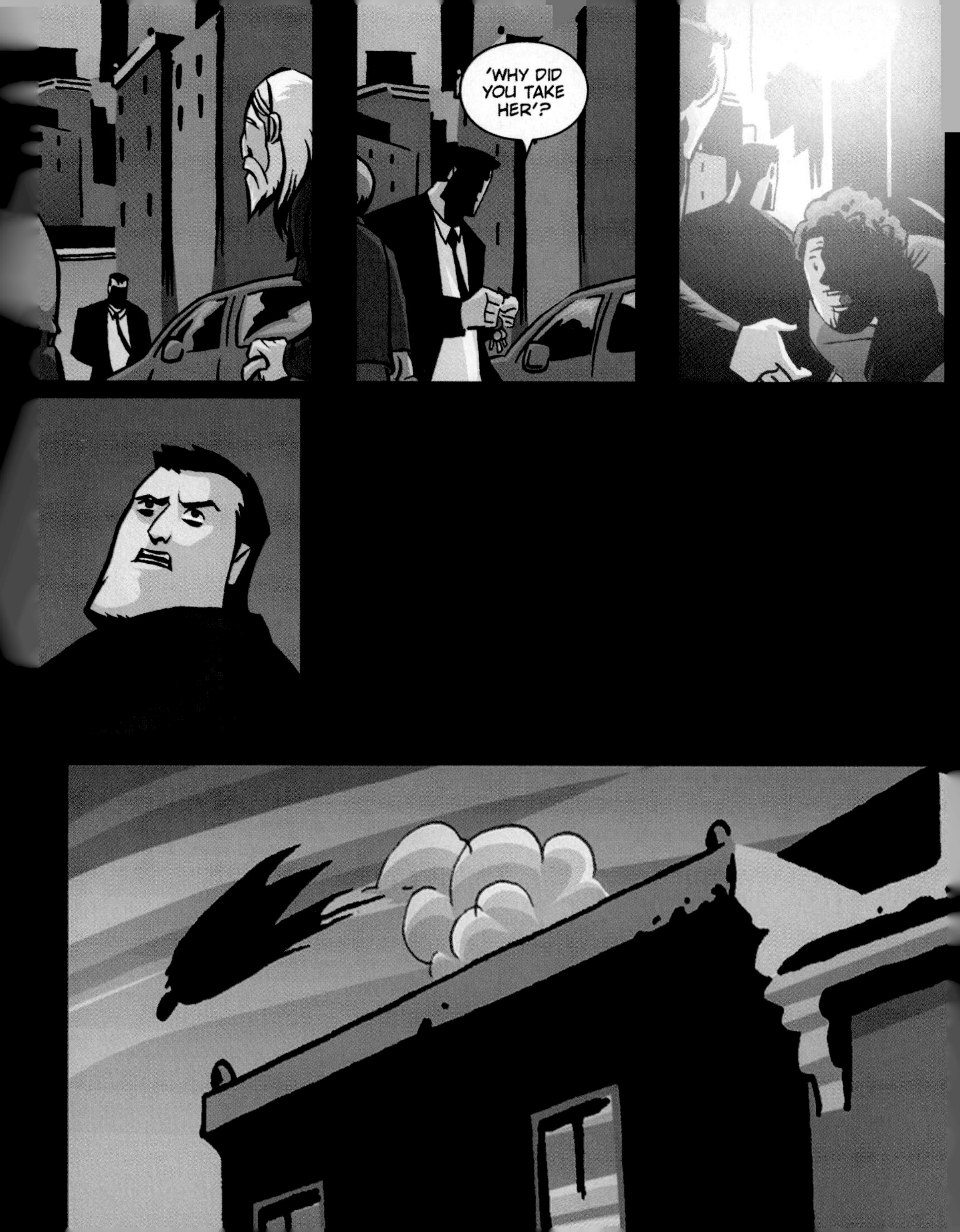
'WHY DID YOU TAKE HER'?

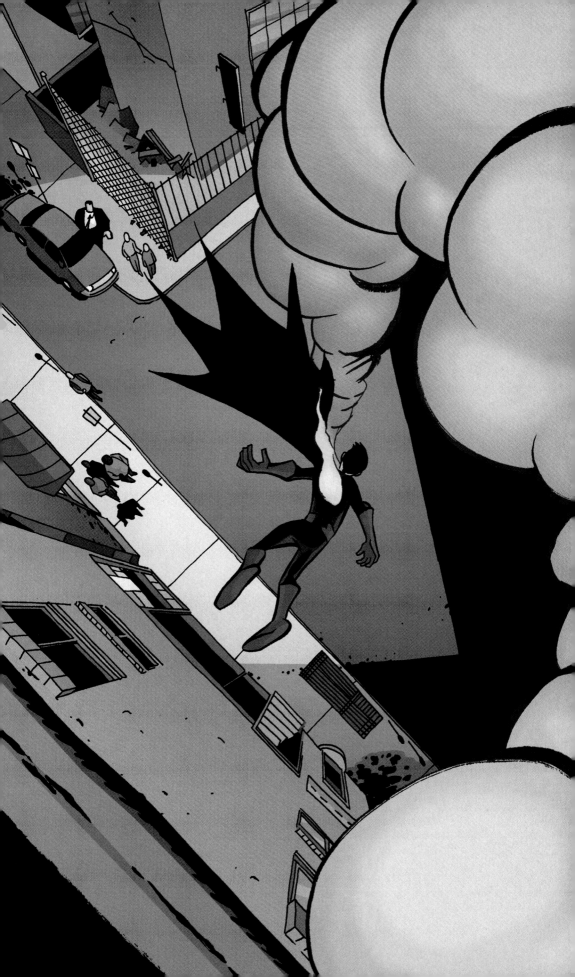

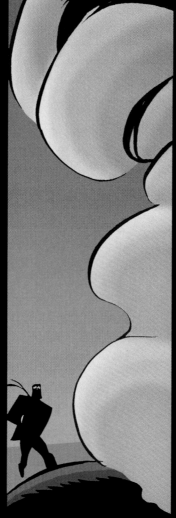

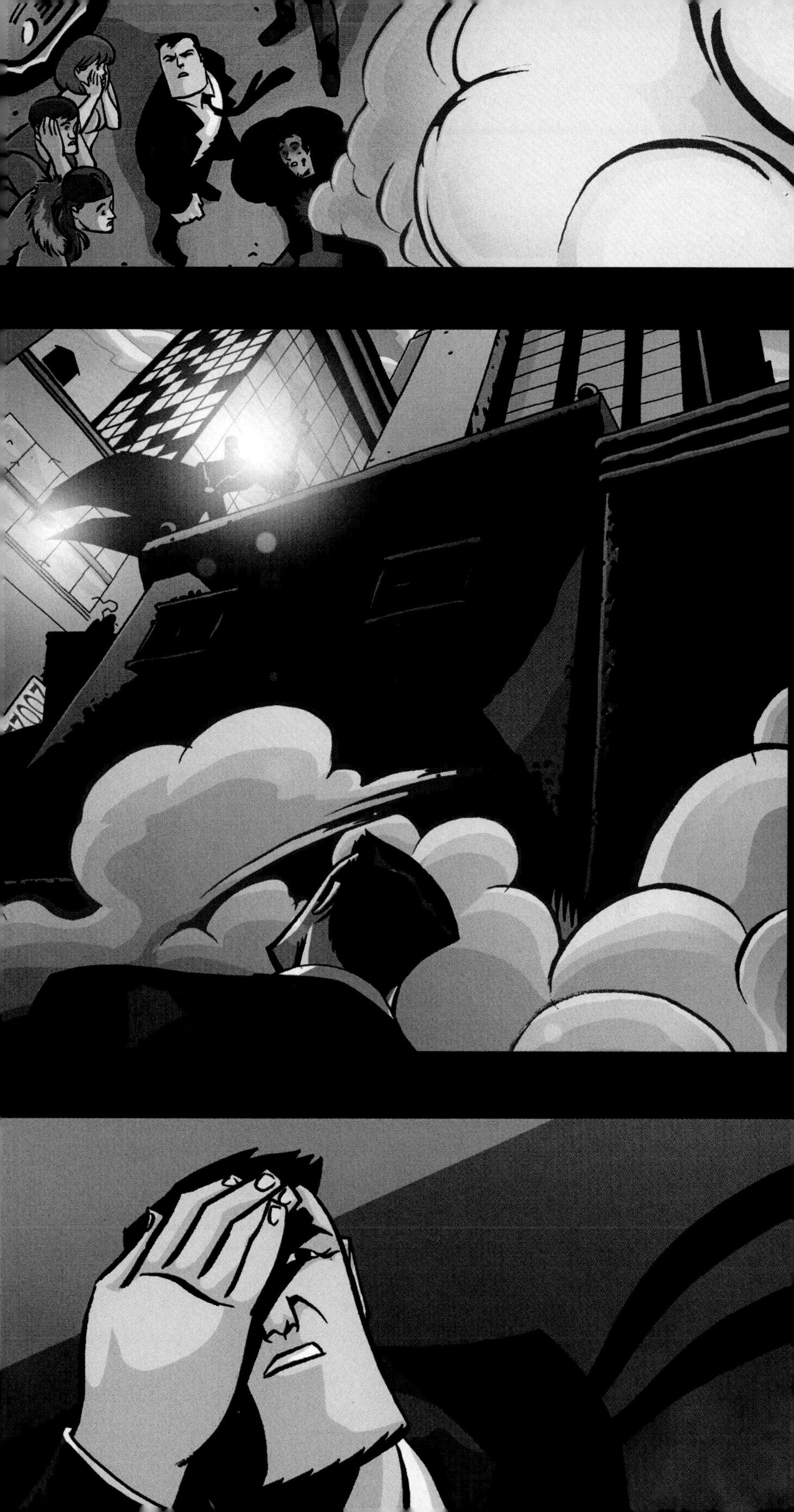

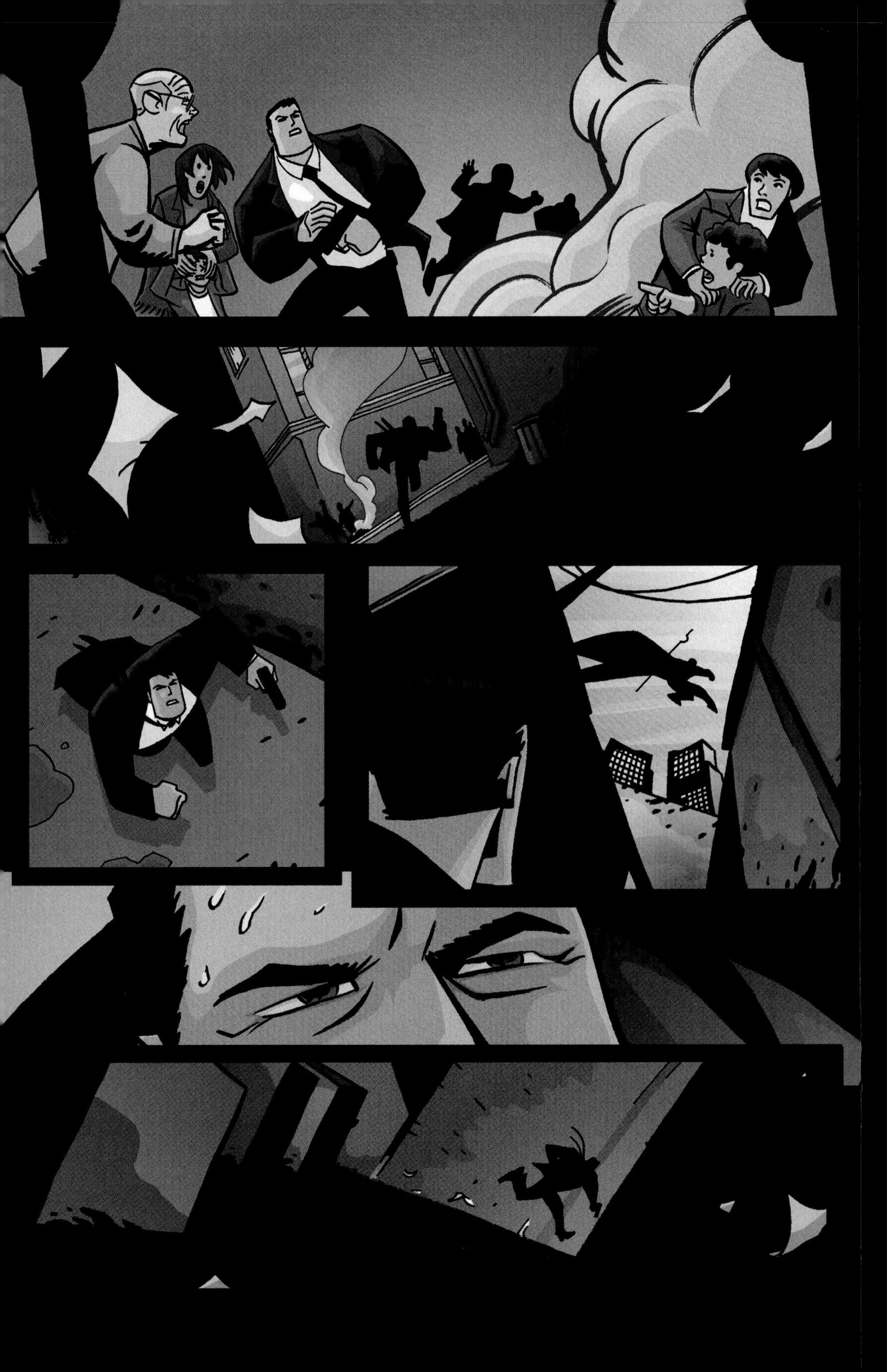

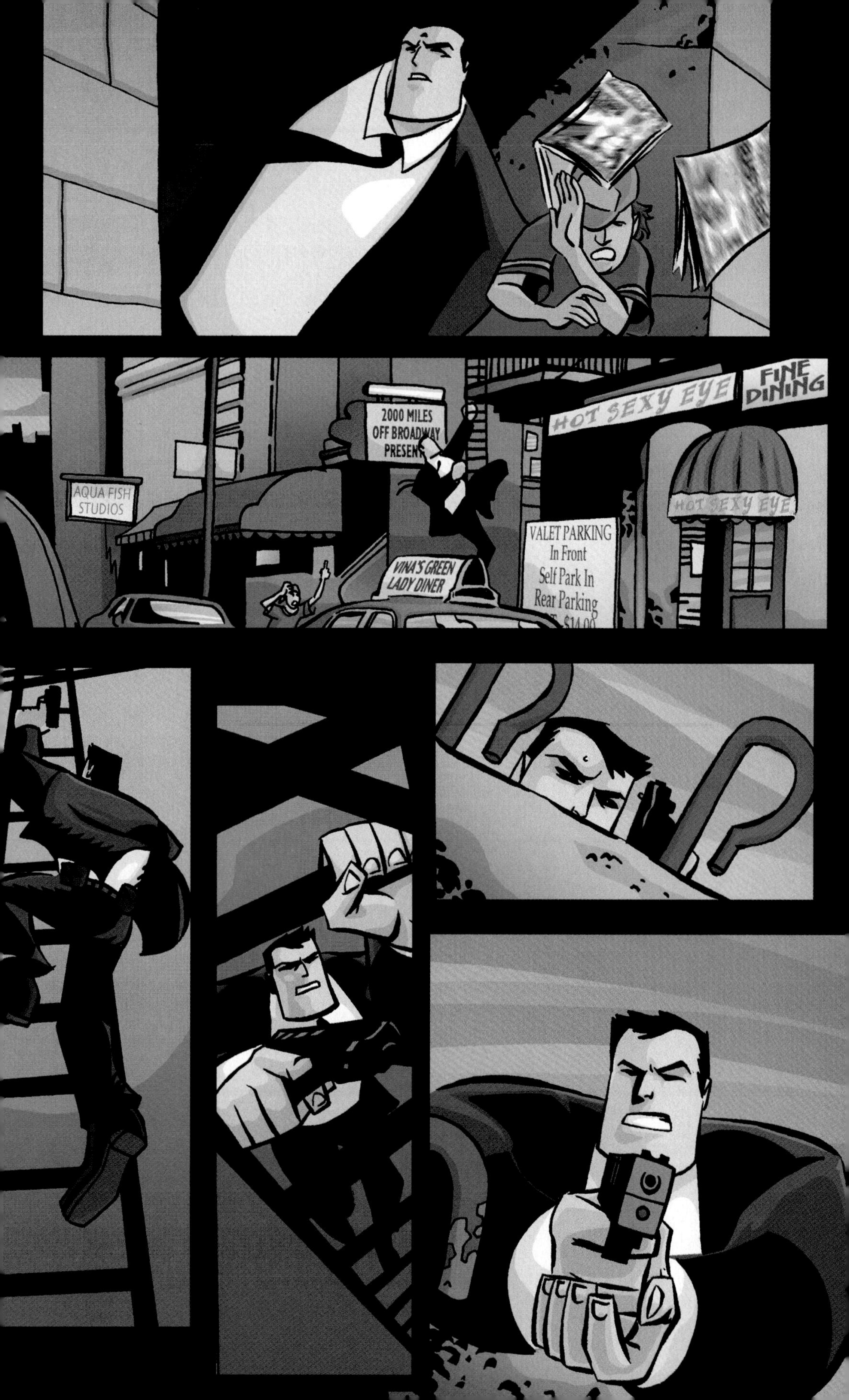

2000 MILES
OFF BROADWAY
PRESENT
HOT SEXY EYE
FINE DINING
AQUA FISH
STUDIOS
HOT SEXY EYE
VALET PARKING
In Front
Self Park In
Rear Parking
VINA'S GREEN
LADY DINER

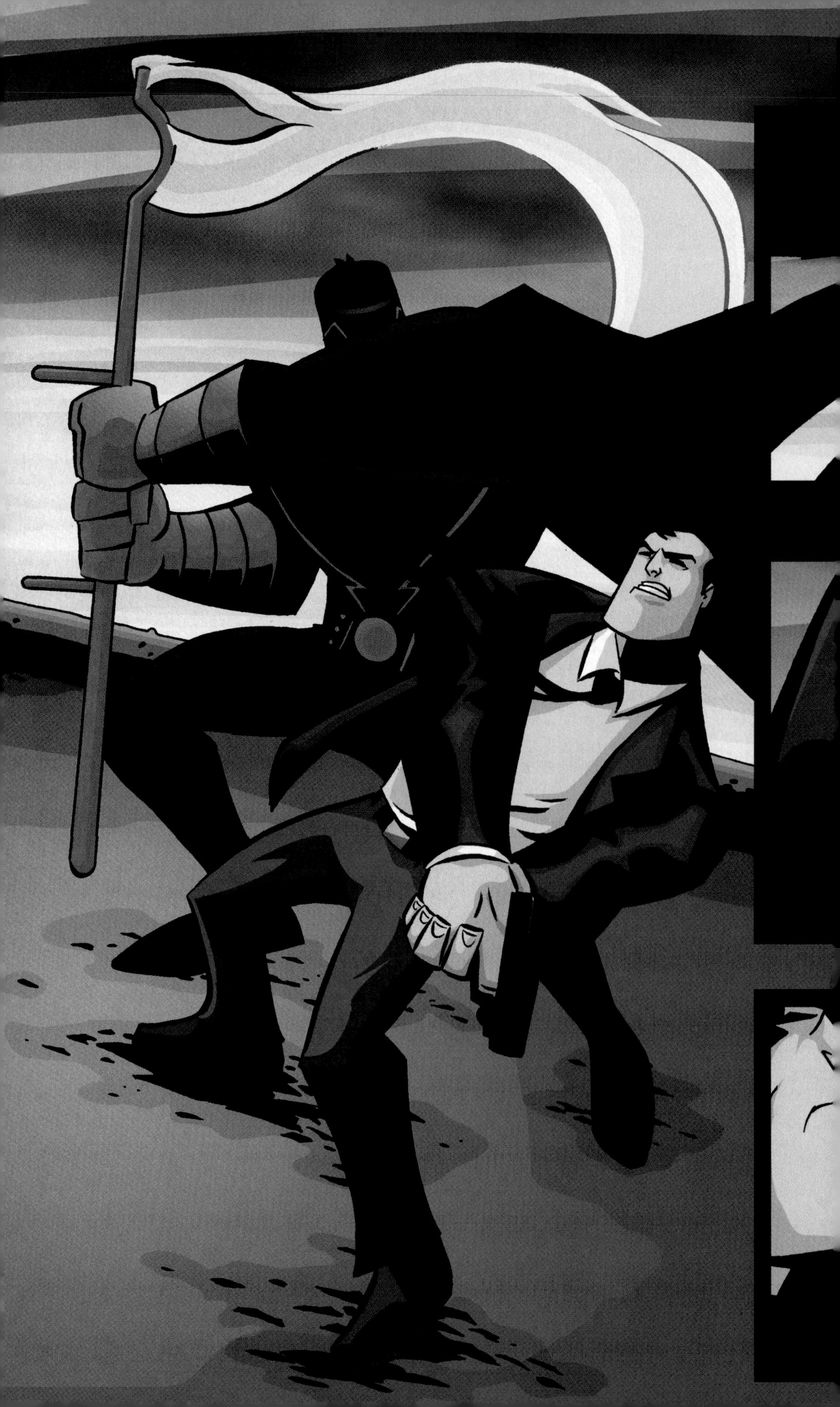

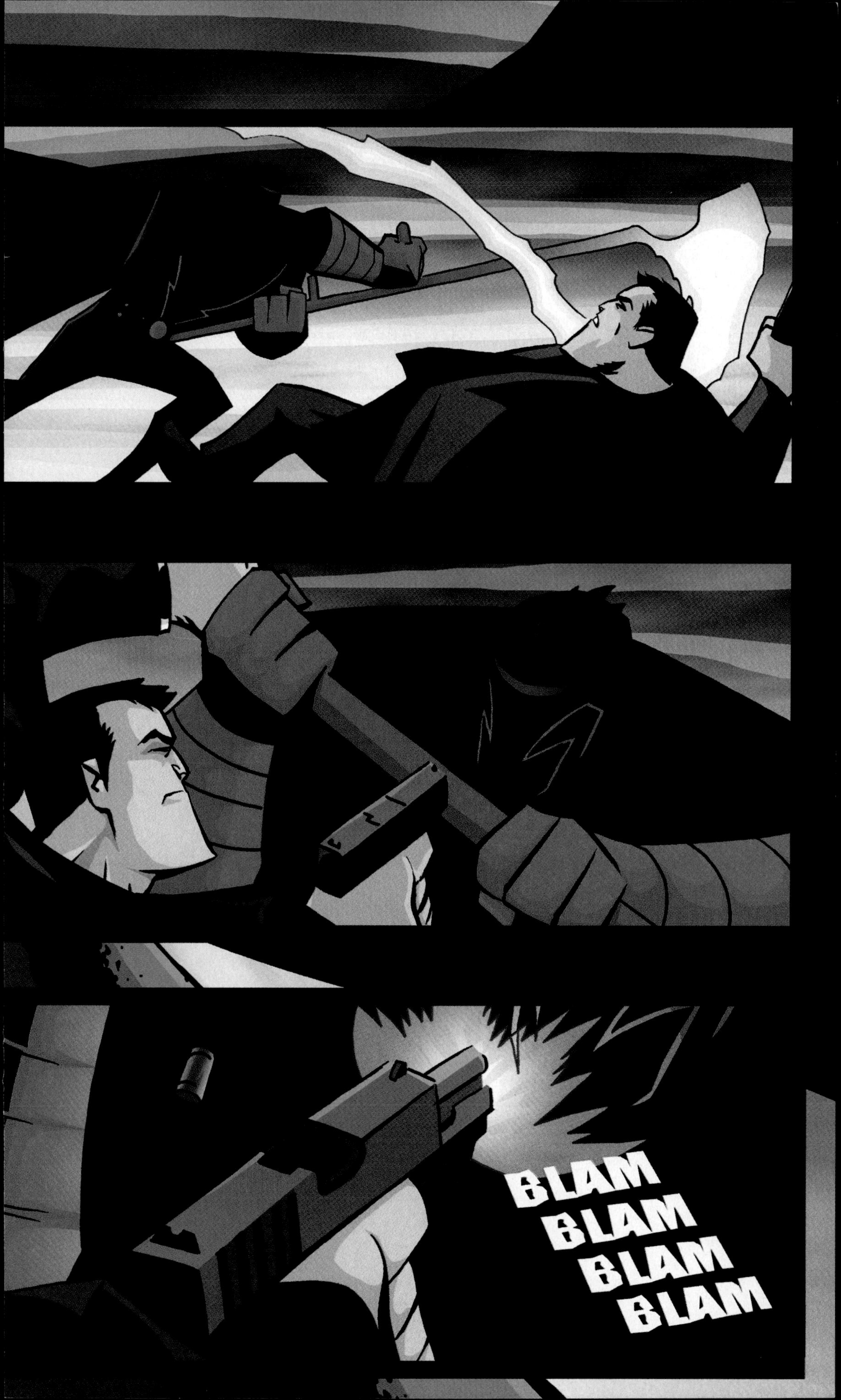
BLAM
BLAM
BLAM
BLAM

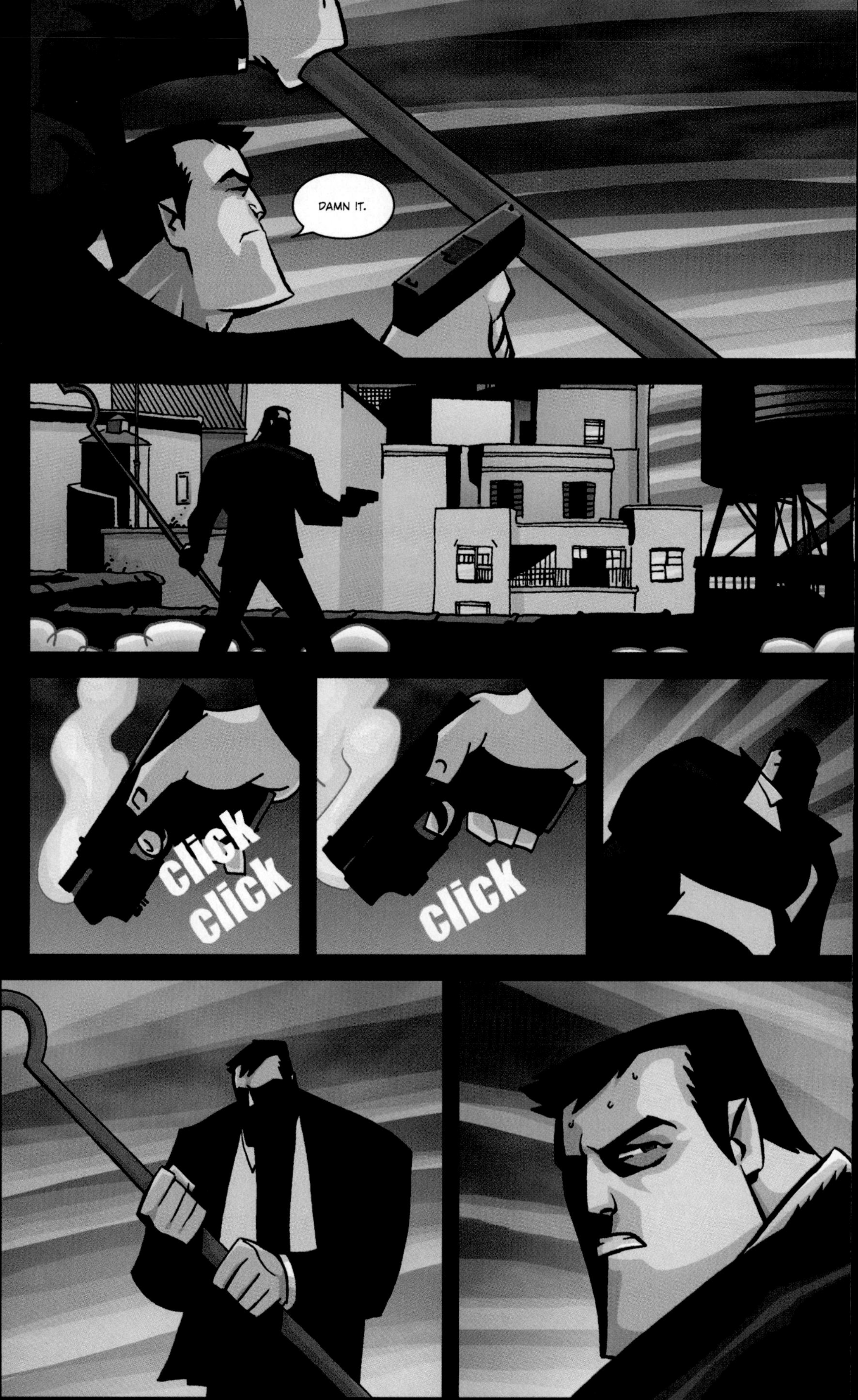
DAMN IT.
click
click
click

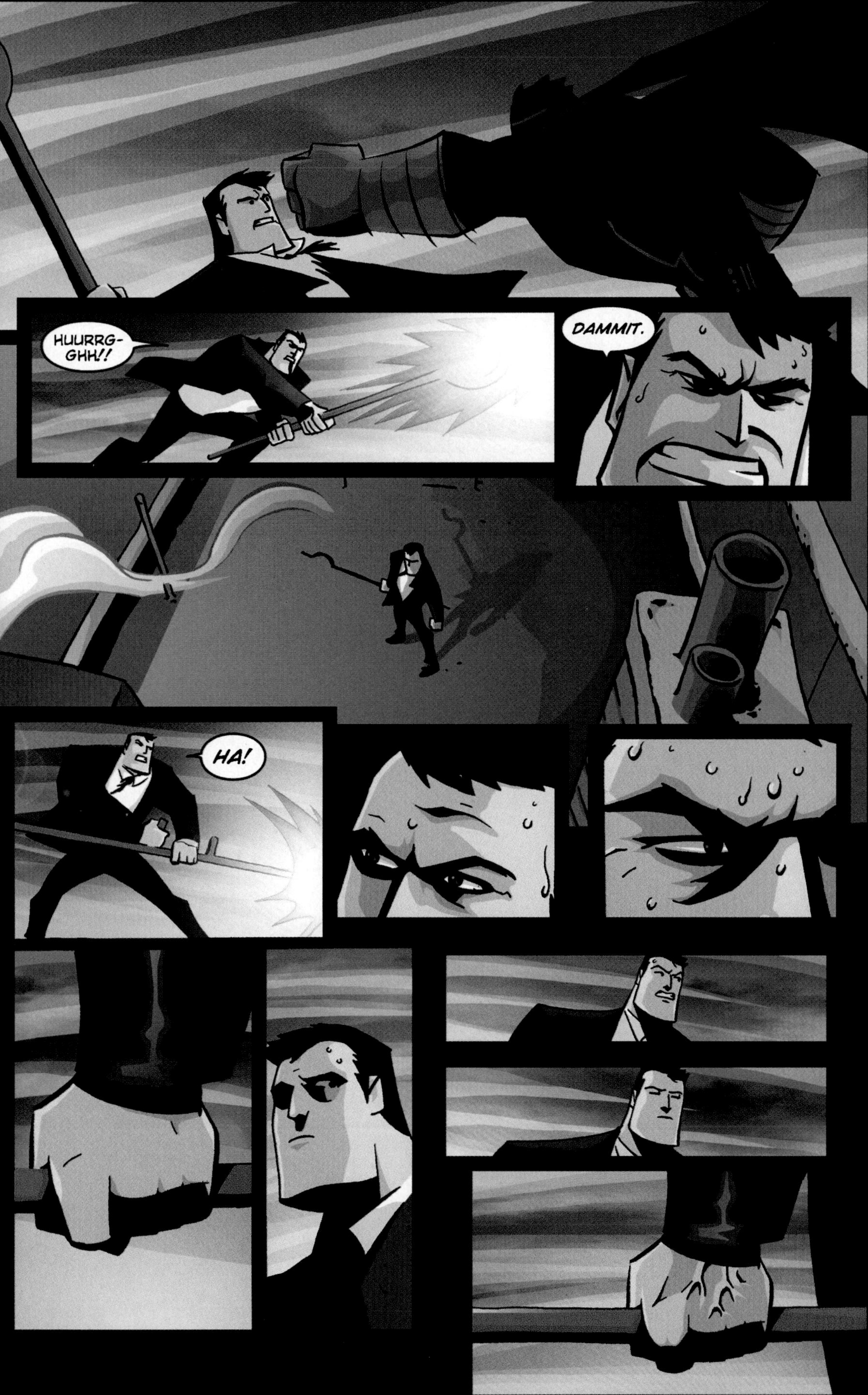
HUURRG-GHH!!
DAMMIT.
HA!

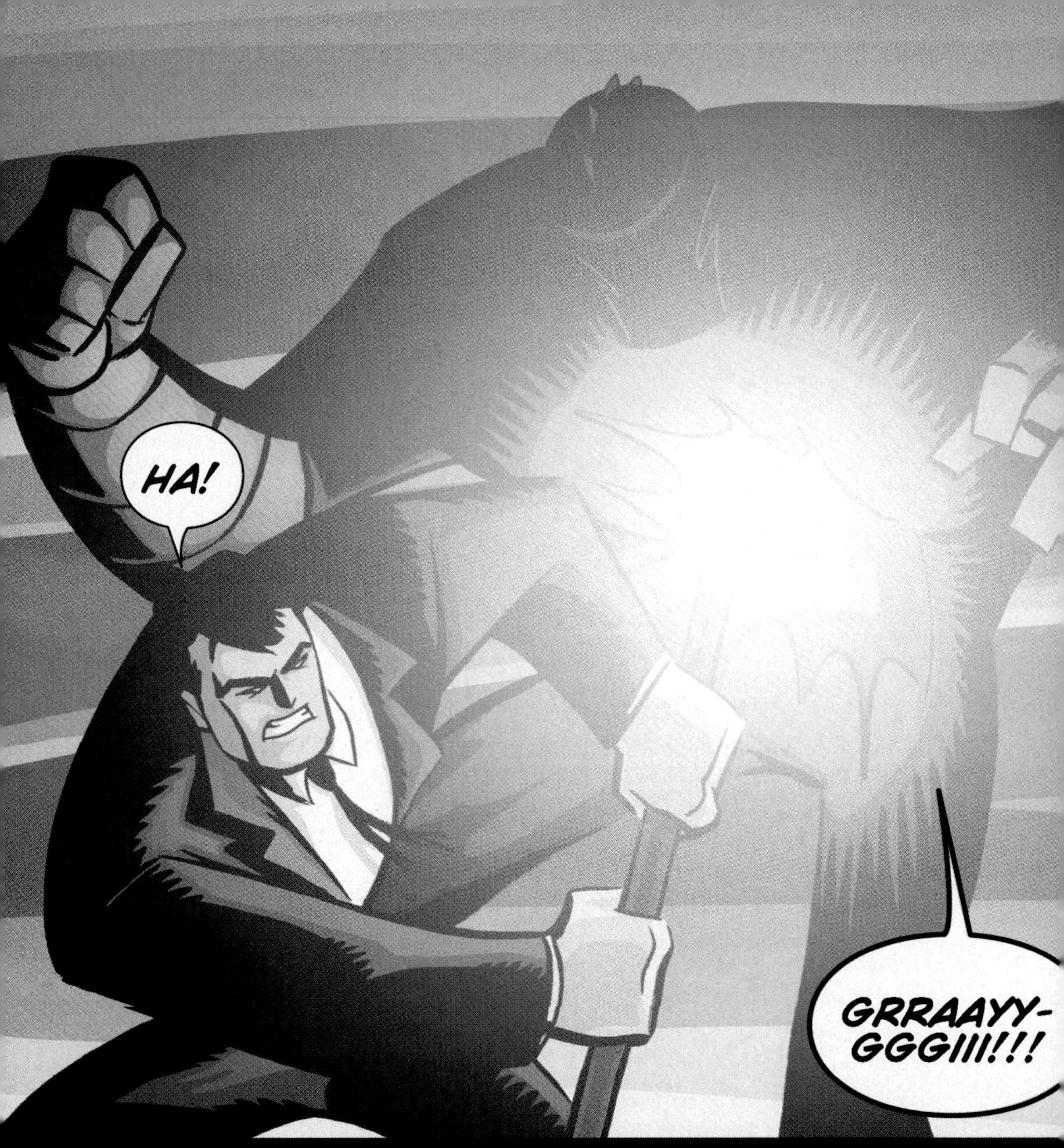
HA!
GRRAAYY-
GGGIII!!!

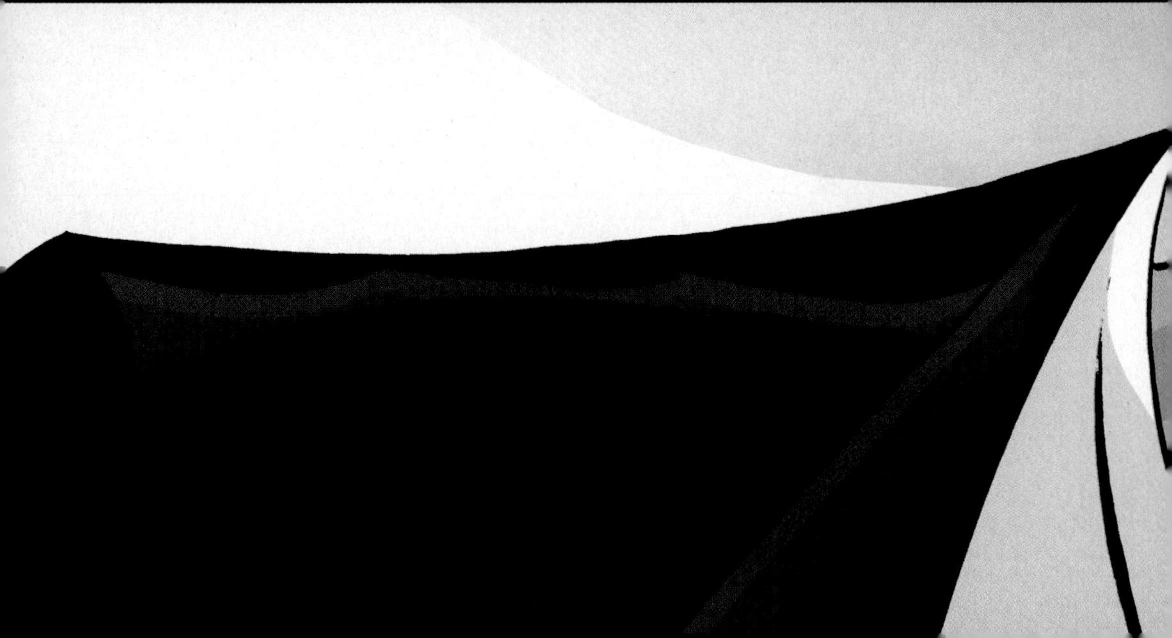

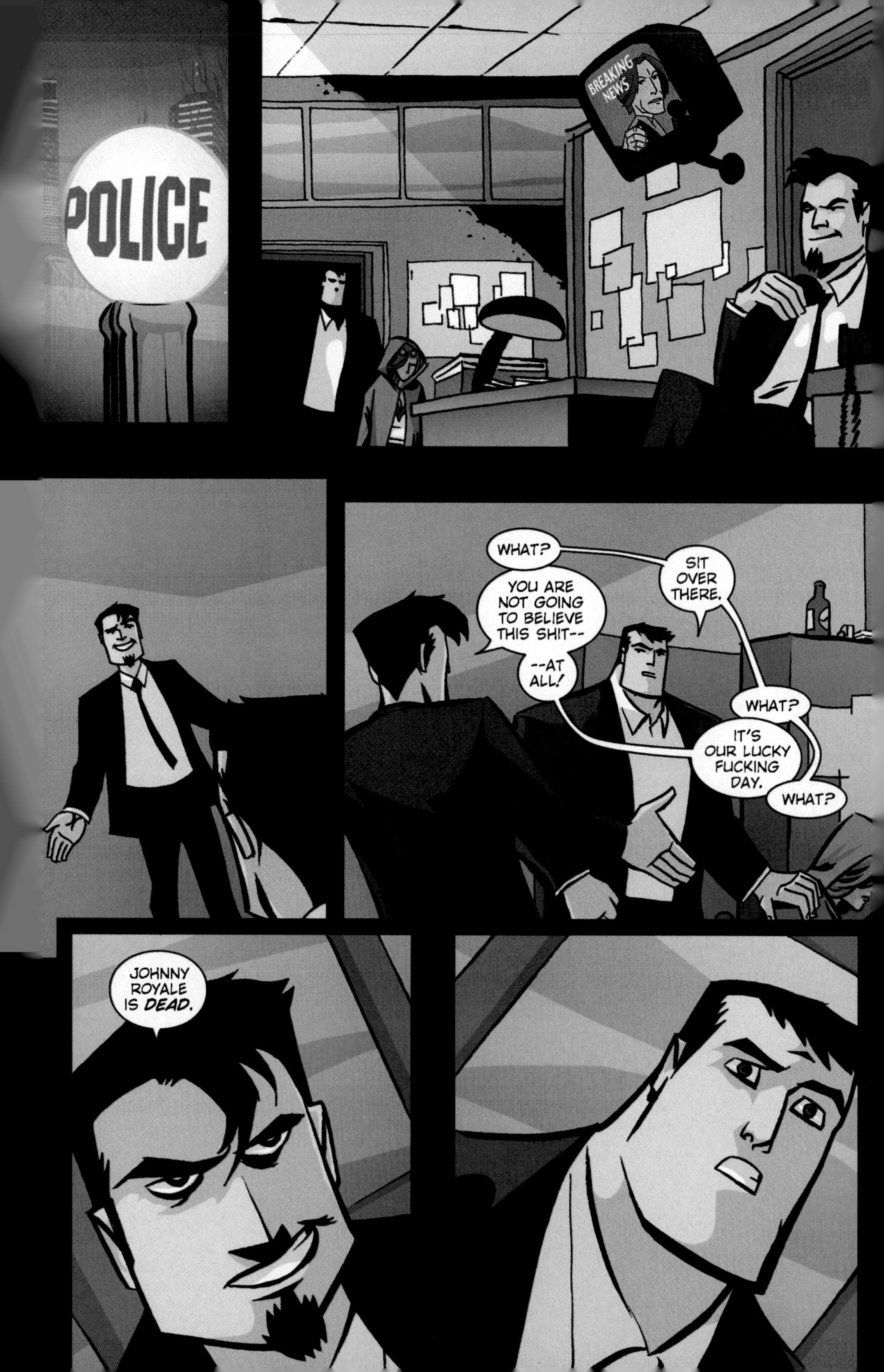
POLICE
BREAKING NEWS
WHAT?
YOU ARE NOT GOING TO BELIEVE THIS SHIT--
SIT OVER THERE.
--AT ALL!
WHAT?
IT'S OUR LUCKY FUCKING DAY.
WHAT?
JOHNNY ROYALE IS *DEAD*.

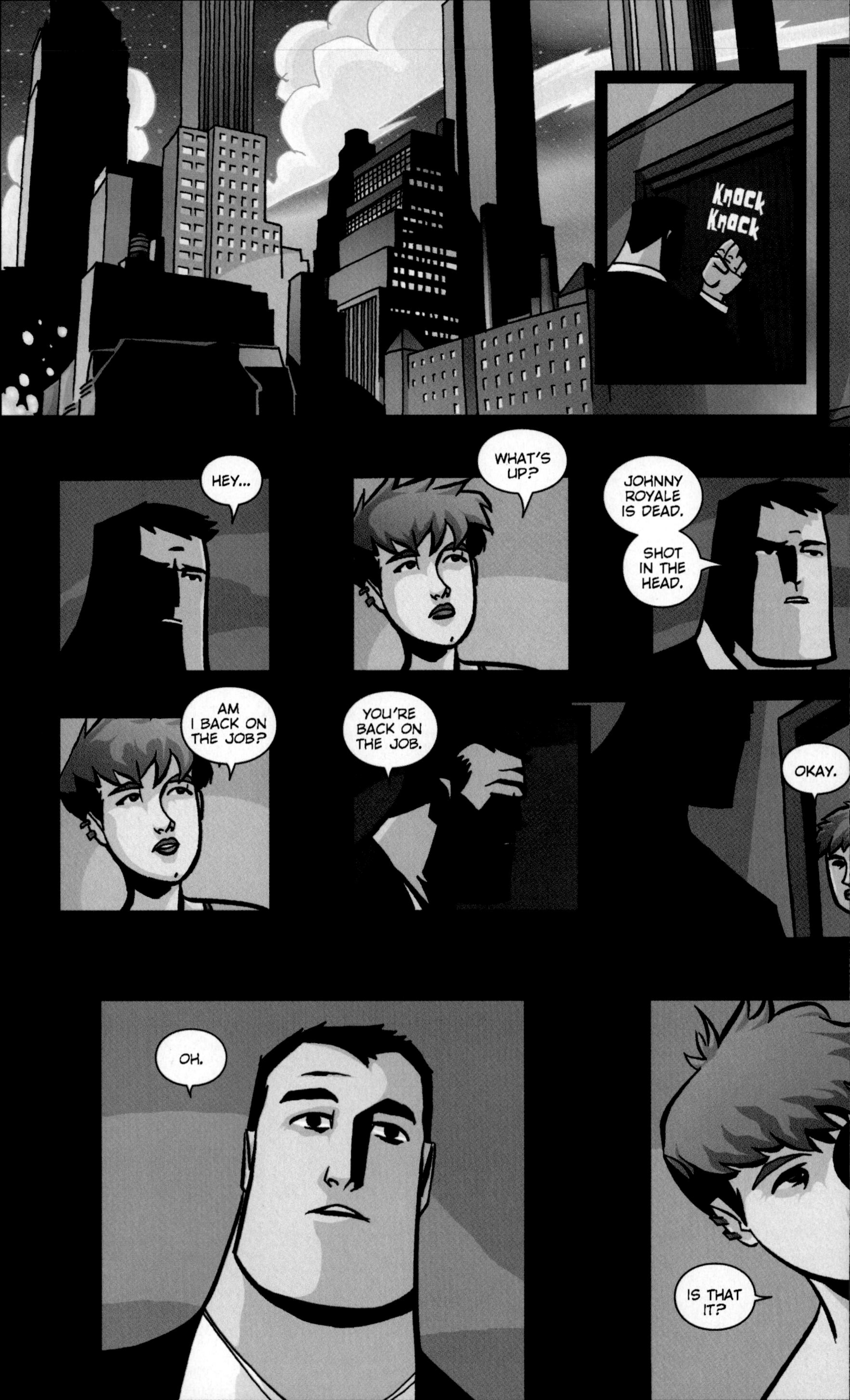
Knock Knock
HEY...
WHAT'S UP?
JOHNNY ROYALE IS DEAD.
SHOT IN THE HEAD.
AM I BACK ON THE JOB?
YOU'RE BACK ON THE JOB.
OKAY.
OH.
IS THAT IT?

POWERS

Anatomy of a cover concept...

Ever notice how there's about five basic mainstream comic book cover designs? You know them:

* The hero leaping at you, readying for battle.
* The close up of the hero grimacing at you, with the shadow of whatever villain he is facing cast half over his face.
* The logo of the comic smashing under the force of the great battle going on underneath it.
* The big maniacally laughing villain close up.
* And lets not forget, the ever popular giant boobs smushed together in the middle of the cover with a couple of spots of blood on them that, at first glance, somewhat resemble nipplage.

These are what we call in the business: Comic Book Cliches. And If I am ever responsible for purposefully executing one here in Powers, I will kill myself, but then make it look like Mike Oeming did it. Mike and I decided very early on to create theme covers for each storyarc. And for this storyline we ended up using album cover designs from albums you would find in a college dorm room.

But the road to a good idea is not always smooth. There's a lot of really bad ideas pursued, or as Mike likes to call them: ideas forced down the artists throat from a know-it-all writer. And then there are the cover designs created by an artist hopped up on paint fumes.

Join us now as we take you on a trip through the cover gallery, then onto the abandoned cover concepts and sketches. We hope that you will find it interesting, and by that I mean I hope the extra effort gets us nominated for something.

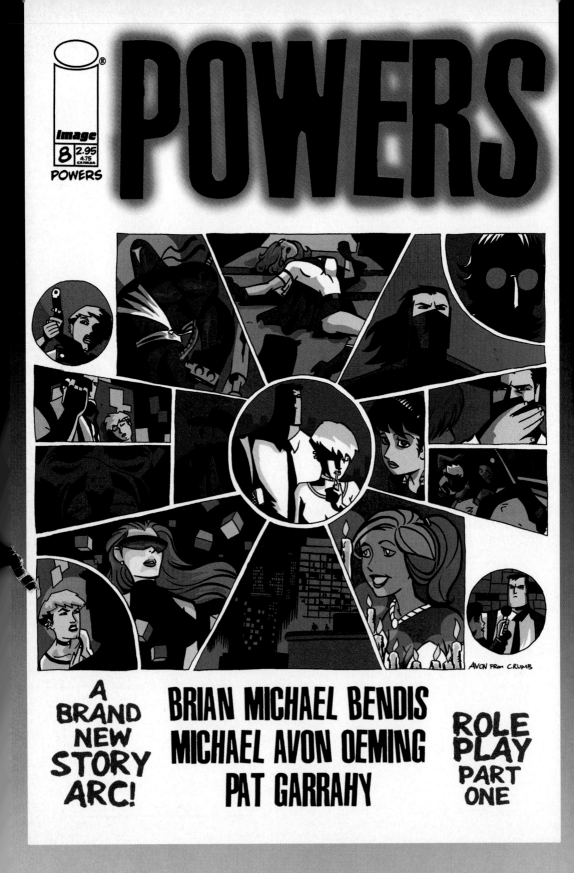

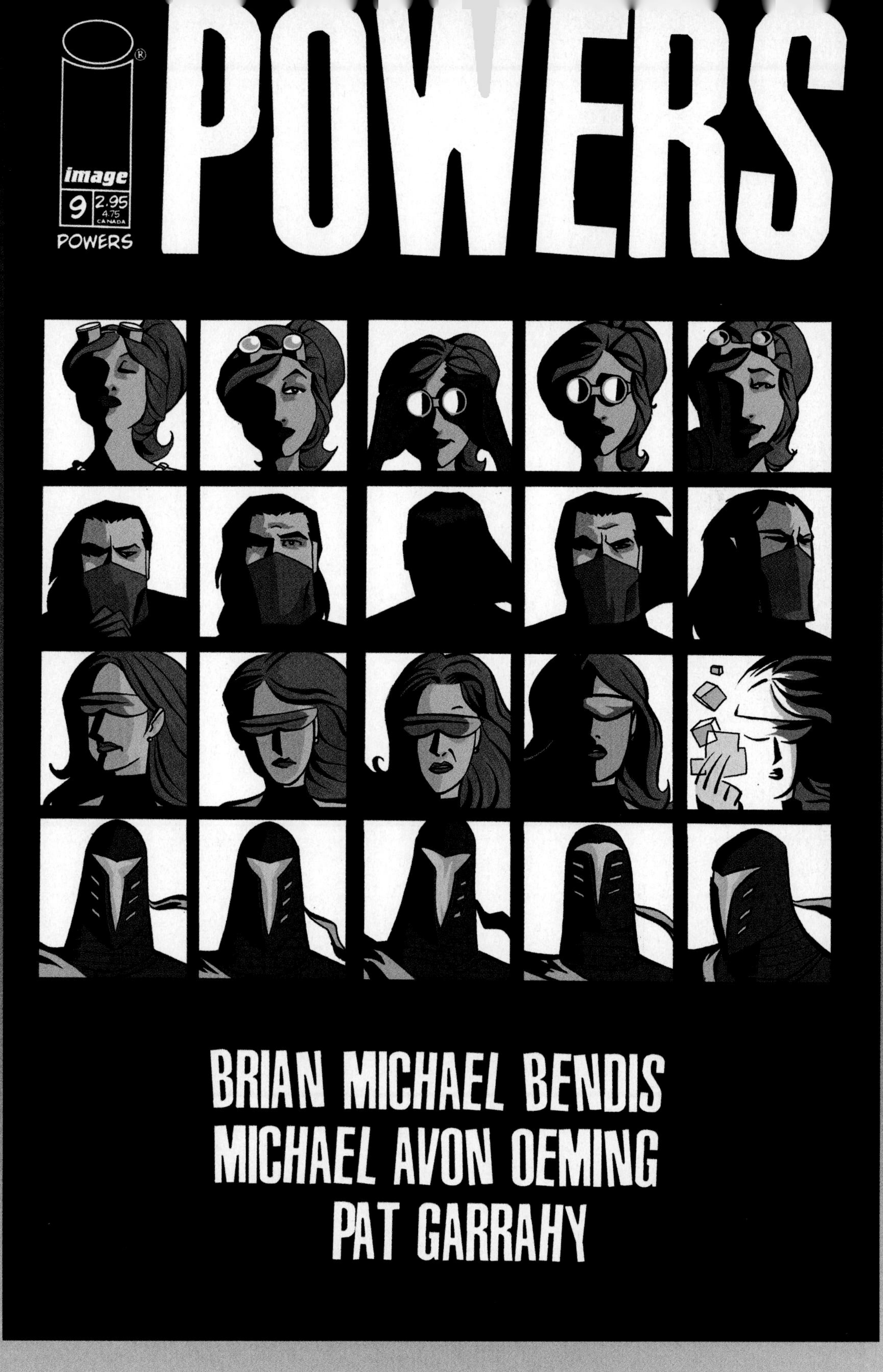
image
9
2.95
4.75 CANADA
POWERS
POWERS
BRIAN MICHAEL BENDIS
MICHAEL AVON OEMING
PAT GARRAHY

The Beatles: A Hard Days Night- British import single

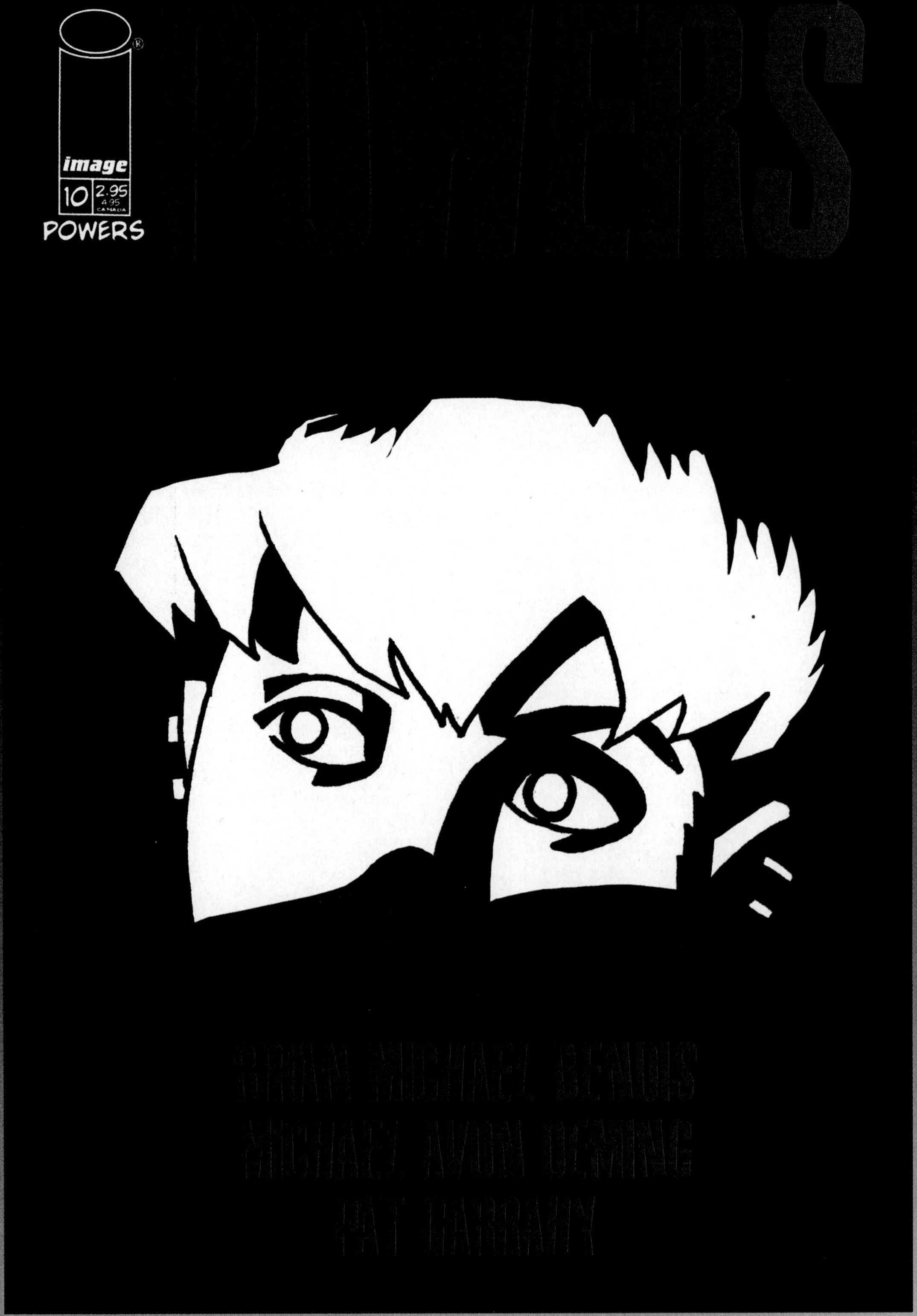

image
10
2.95
4.95 CANADA
POWERS
POWERS
BRIAN MICHAEL BENDIS
MICHAEL AVON OEMING
PAT GARRAHY

Sinead O'Connor: I Do Not Want What I Haven't Got

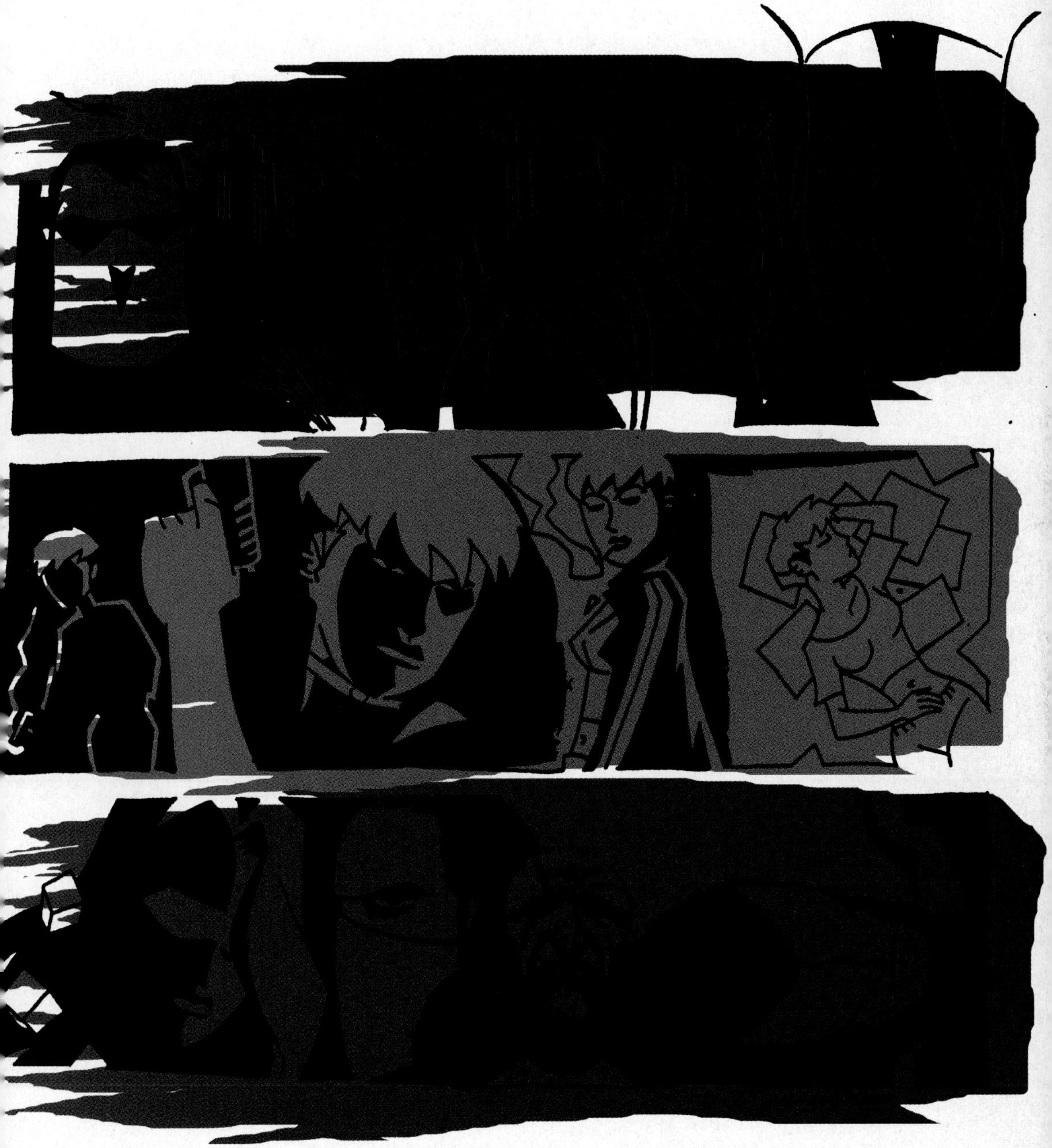

Abandoned cover for Powers 10 based on the Police: Syncronicity

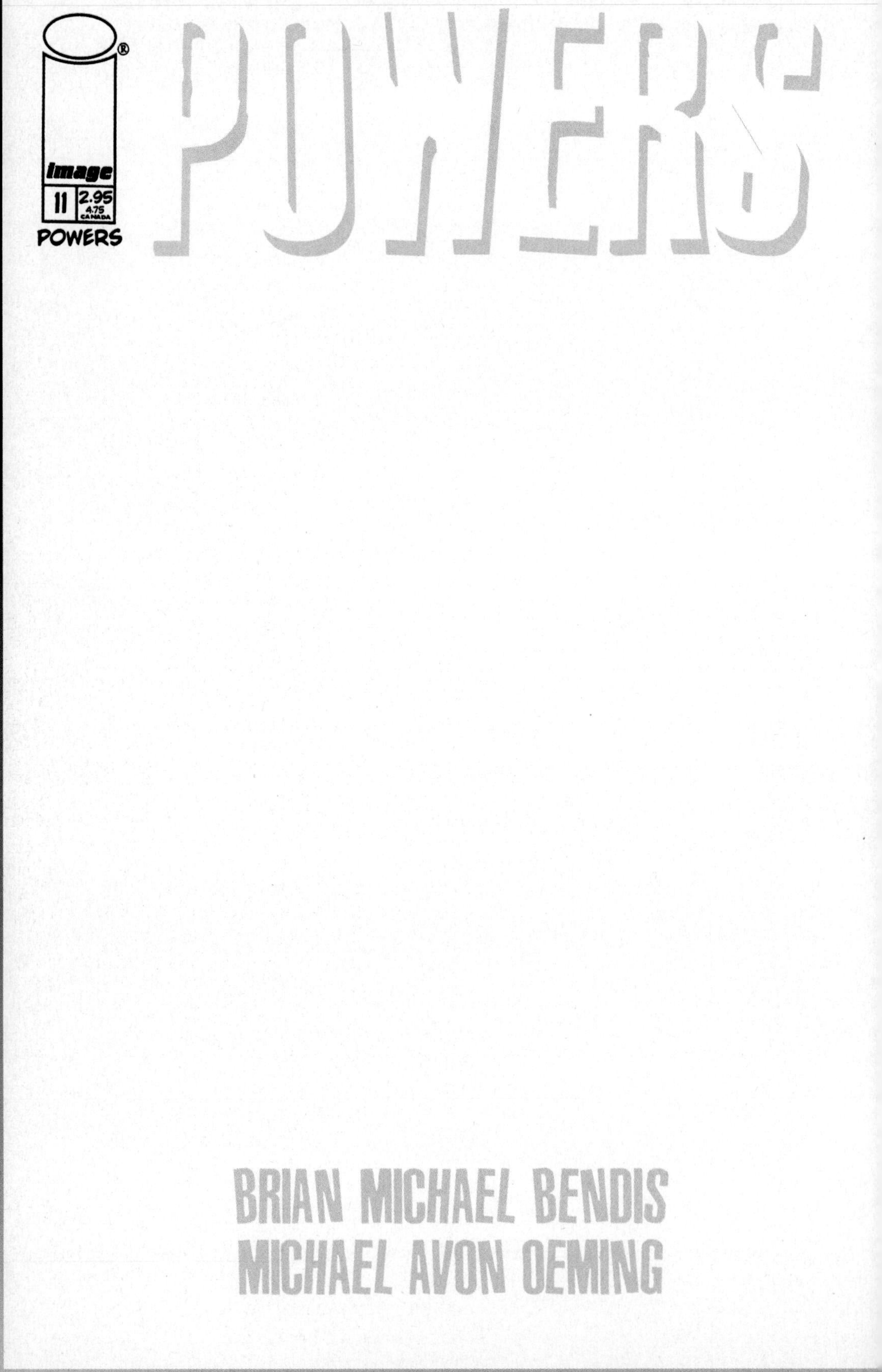
image
11 2.95 4.75 CANADA
POWERS
POWERS
BRIAN MICHAEL BENDIS
MICHAEL AVON OEMING

The Beatles: White Album (Duh…)

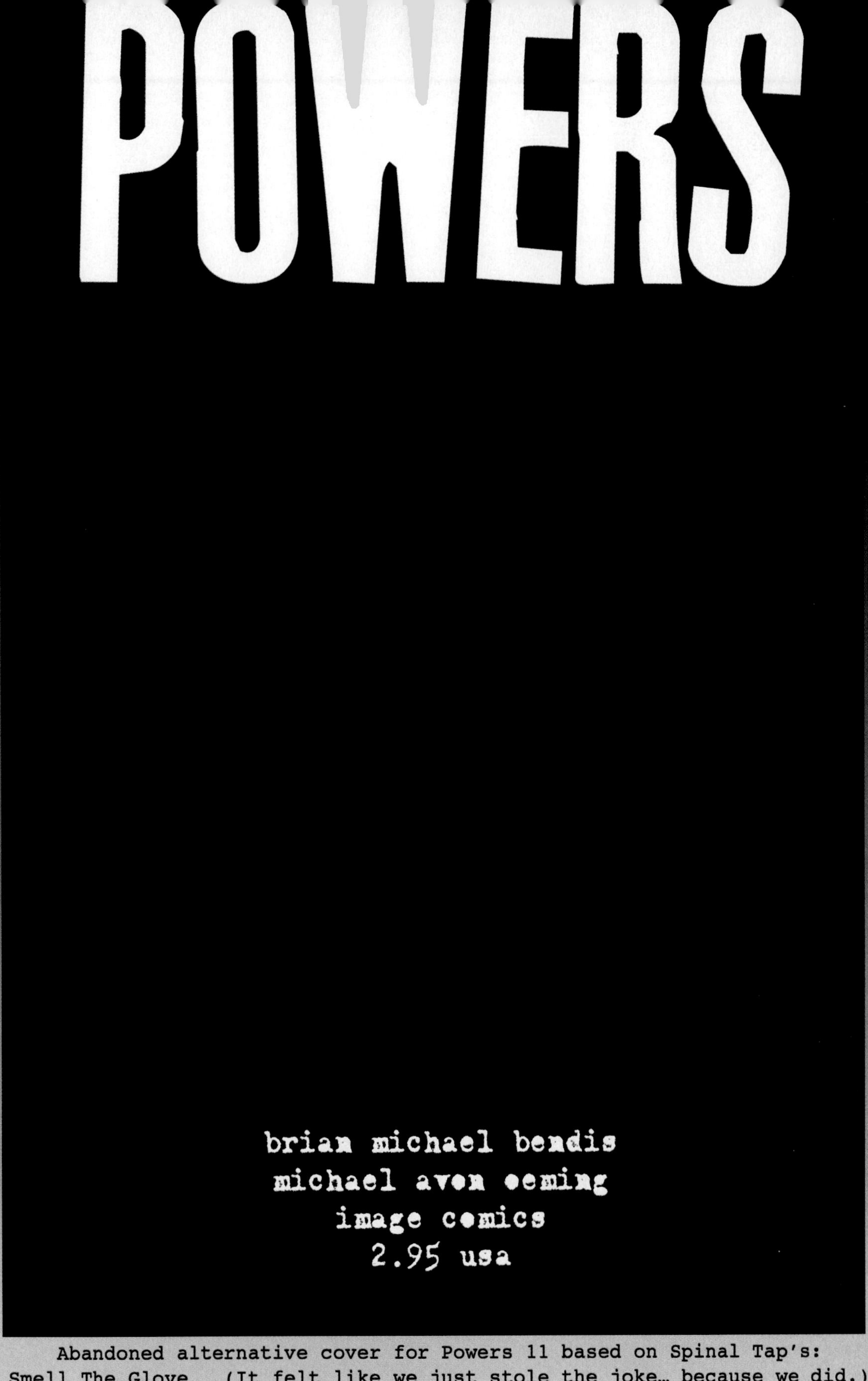
POWERS
brian michael bendis
michael avon oeming
image comics
2.95 usa

Abandoned alternative cover for Powers 11 based on Spinal Tap's:
Smell The Glove (It felt like we just stole the joke… because we did.)

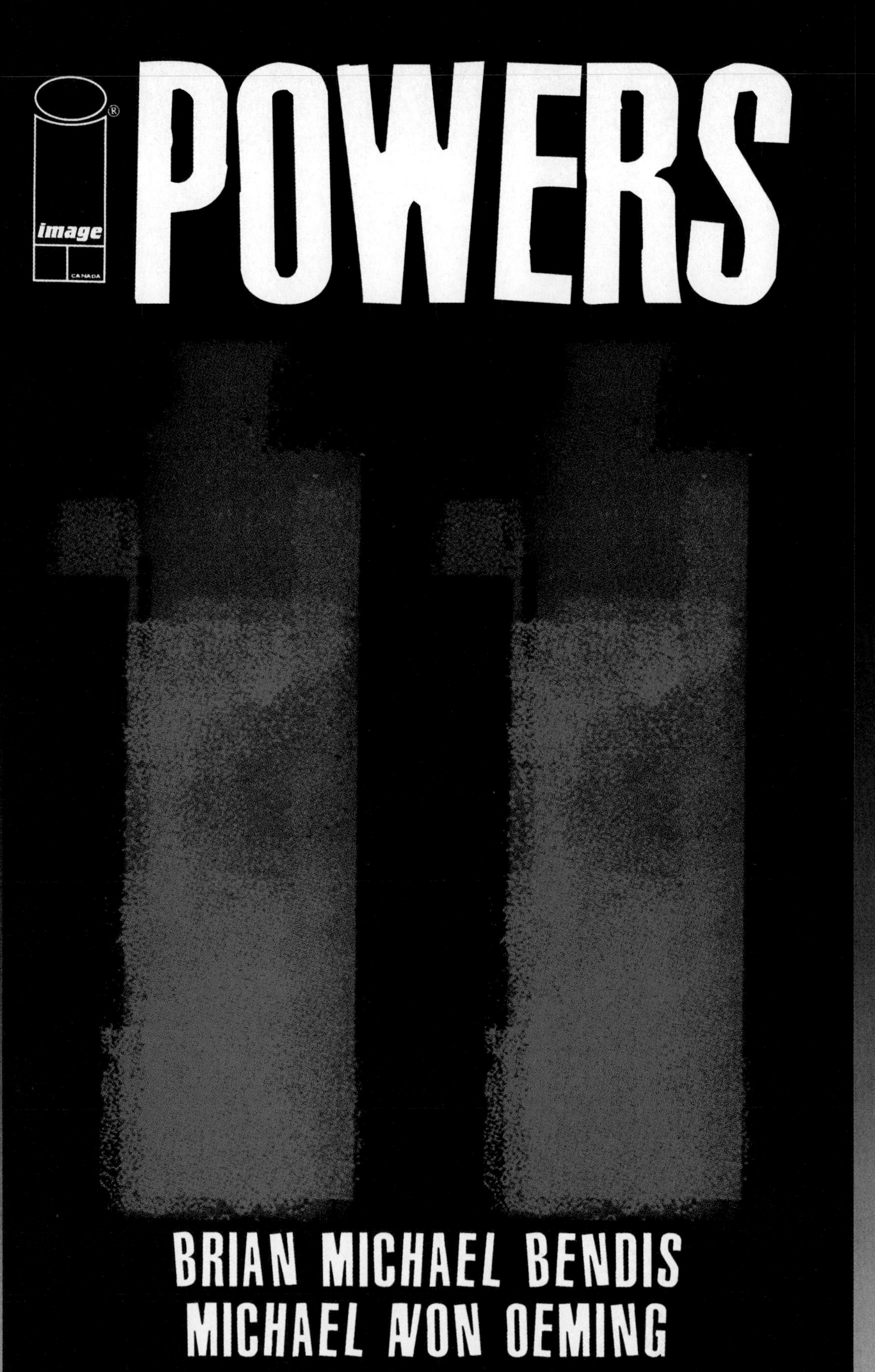
image
CANADA
POWERS
BRIAN MICHAEL BENDIS
MICHAEL AVON OEMING

Abandoned cover for Powers 11 based on The Beatles: One Album
(It felt like we just stole the artwork and altered it…because we did.)

POWERS

THE EISNER AWARD WINNER

Abandoned cover designs for Powers using graphics instead of an image. Not a bad idea but badly produced and it has nothing to do with the storyline.

FROM THE WRITER OF ULTIMATE SPIDER-MAN

FROM THE ARTIST OF BLUNTMAN AND CHRONIC

ROLEPLAY

BENDIS   OEMING

POWERS POWERS POW

POWERS POWERS

A BOOK YOU MUS READ!
– WIZARD

POWERS POWERS POW

ERS POWERS

FROM THE WRITER OF ULTIMATE SPIDER-MAN

PO

POWERS POWERS POW

ERS POWERS POWERS

S

RECOMMENDED TO ANYONE WHO BREATHES!
–COMICS INTERNATIONAL

POWERS POW

RS POWERS POWERS

OWERS POWERS

A PERFECT COMIC BOO
–FANDOM.COM

BENDIS
OEMING
GARRAHY

POWERS POWER

OWERS

WWW.JINXWORLD.COM

POWERS

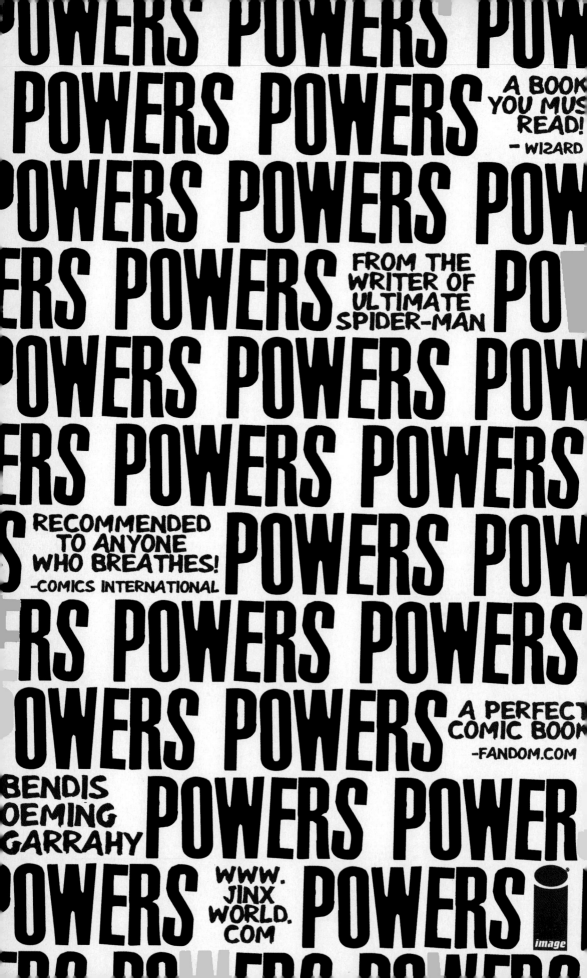

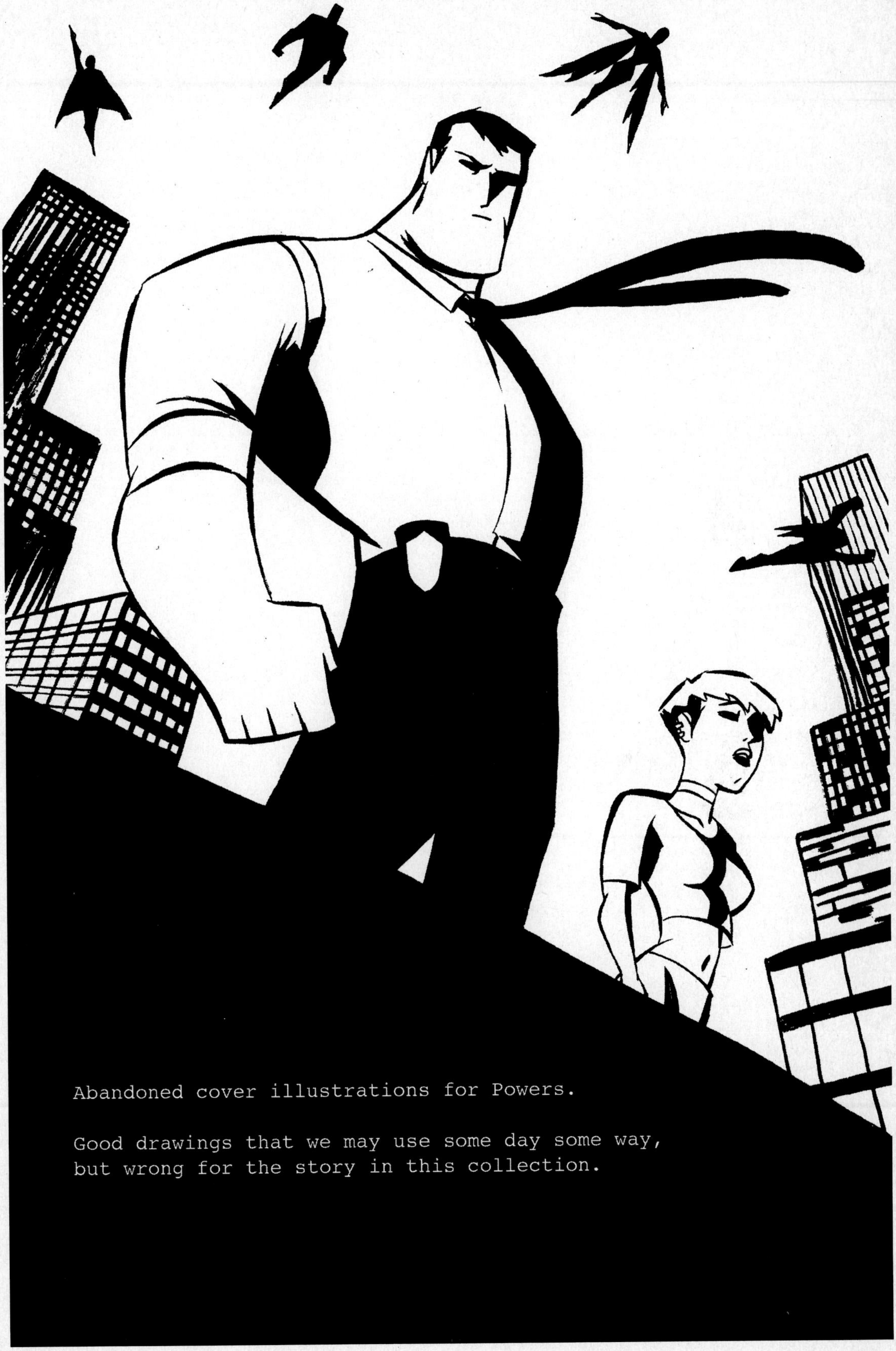

Abandoned cover illustrations for Powers.

Good drawings that we may use some day some way, but wrong for the story in this collection.

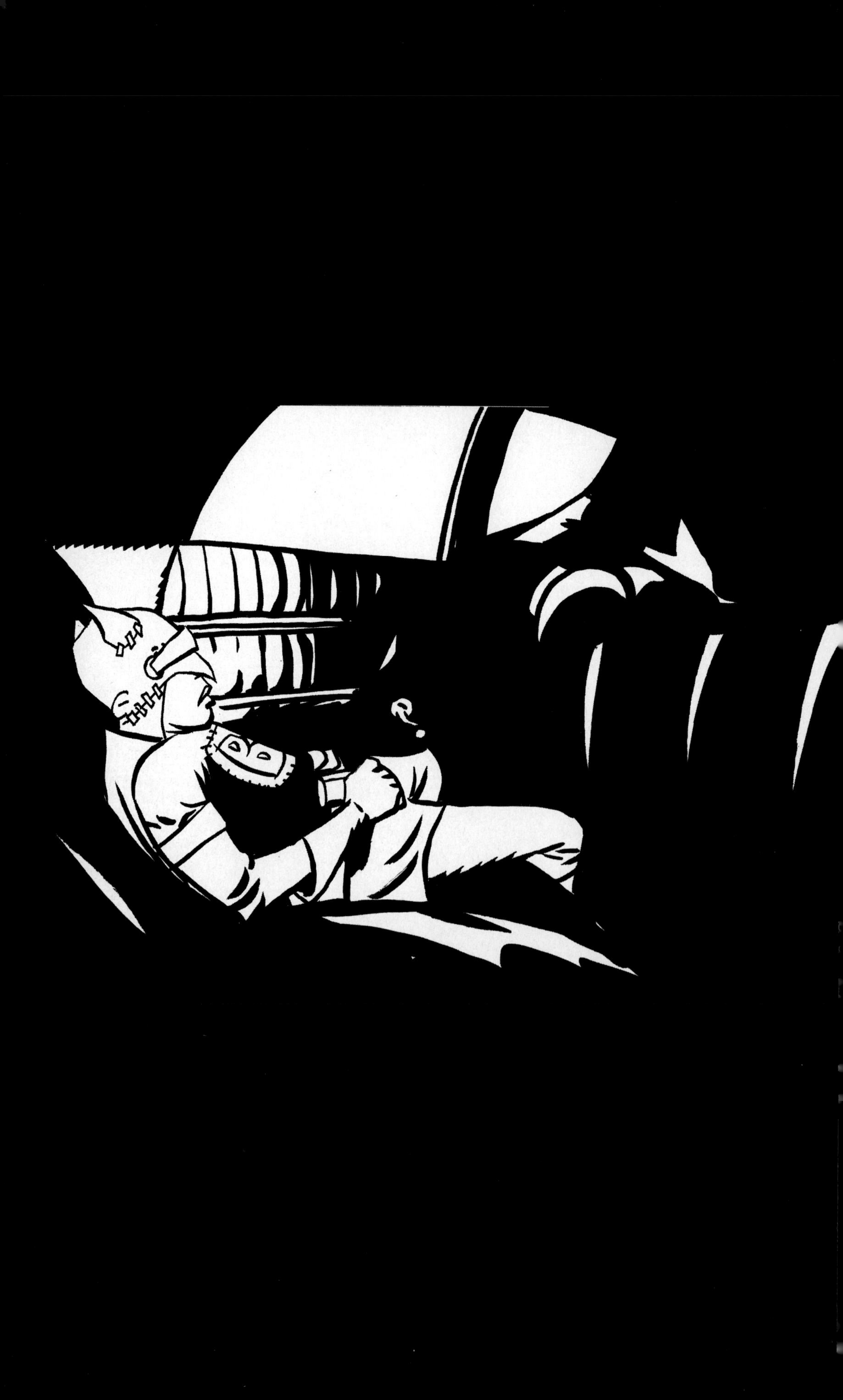

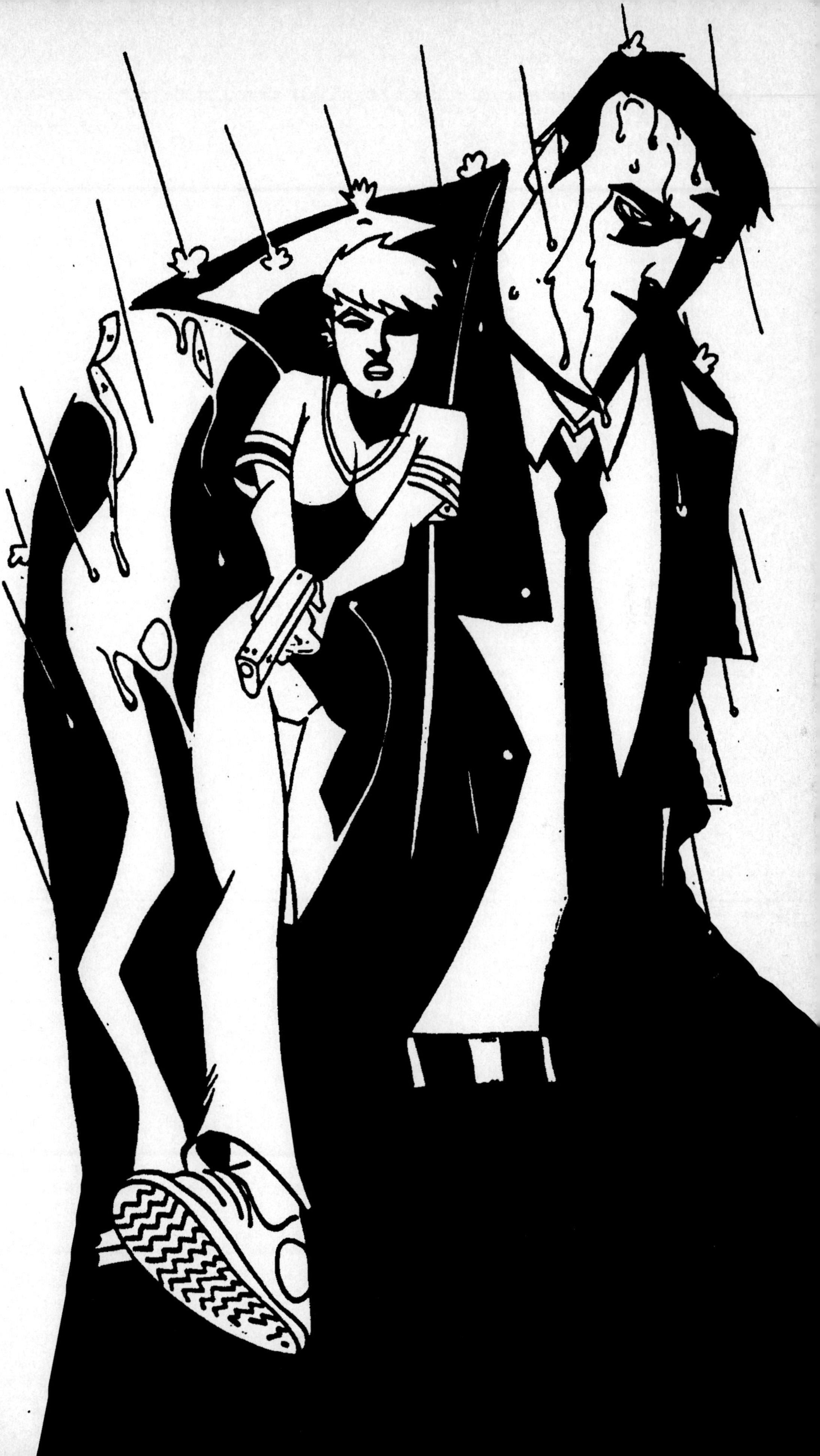

"POWERS" THAT BE:
Five Minutes With Mike Oeming

One of the hottest, most intriguing comics out there right now is *Powers*, a book
that's taken the industry by storm. Following the beat of two human detectives
investigating "powers-related" crimes in their superhuman world, *Powers* escaped from
the minds of writer Brian Michael Bendis, who has had his own success as writer/artist
with *a.k.a. Goldfish* and *Jinx*, and artist Michael Avon Oeming, who's work on *Ship of
Fools* caught him more attention after his work on books like *Judge Dredd* and his
superhero work.

The stylistic approach to *Powers* is very specific; in fact, Mike Oeming notes it was
the impetus behind getting together with Brian Michael Bendis and specifically
creating a crime comic.

"I met Brian Bendis years ago when he was doing store signings for *a.k.a. Goldfish*. We
just clicked right away," Oeming relates. "We stayed in touch and talked about working
together. After different projects came and went, I was looking for something new to
do. I called Brian and was like, 'I want to do a crime book and I want to use this
particular kind of style'-- this Bruce Timm-ish /Alex Toth kind of animated stuff. And
I really wanted to use it in a crime thing."

The artist explains the development of the realistic animated look of *Powers*. "The
style developed from my trying to get work on the *Batman Adventures* stuff. I liked
that style, but I couldn't stay on model, because I saw other things it had potential
for that the series wasn't quite allowing. I really like stuff Timm was influenced by,
specifically Alex Toth who was a *huge* influence on me. I just wanted to do some crime
stuff using a combination of their two styles.

"That's basically what I told Brian," as Oeming affects a begging tone to his voice
and says, "'I want to do a crime book with you 'cause you're a good writer.' And he
was like, 'Absolutely!' We mulled over things. I faxed him some ideas. I didn't care
what it was; I knew that we would just have fun on it. When it started out, all we
were looking to do was a black and white crime book. I assumed that it would be one
issue or a couple of issues that would be released through Image central as a black
and white. At the time, I had just been doing *Ship of Fools* and he was still doing. So
that's all we thought: little, tiny black and white book.

"It just kind of blossomed from there," Oeming explains. "Brian basically had *Powers*
in its nutshell. He showed me the thing and I was hesitant at first. I wanted to do a
straightforward crime thing. And I was like, 'What's this?' And he said, 'No, no it's
not about the heroes!' So even *I* took some convincing and thank God I saw his way!"

Of course, as everyone is well aware — or if you're not, you are now — that little,
tiny black and white book is a bit bigger. Oeming for one is taken by surprise by the
success.

"I'm not sure why it happened," Oeming admits of the sudden hit. "I think a lot of it
had to do with Bendis' fans. He's been doing these crime books for many years now.
First it was *a.k.a Goldfish*, which ran into *Jinx*, which ran into Torso, and then he
stared getting picked up for other companies to do books, like *Sam & Twitch*. So he
really started building this fan base. So that and the commerciality of my artwork, it
was what people were looking for, or at least people who hadn't read his stuff before.
I think that's what I brought into the fold really, was a certain amount of
commerciality. My work's very iconic, you look at it and immediately know what it is,
it's so simple. That's what I like about it. Brian's artwork is more realistic but
both show the same elements of the noir, the use of blacks and lighting. Even though
physically, the artwork *looks* very different, if you look at the pacing, the lighting,
we're working the same way, just in slightly different elements."

bendis as a writer/artist has a unique way of telling his stories for Oeming, and that system works out very well. "His scripts are completely visual which works because we're on the same page, no pun intended," the artist says. "We know exactly what the other is thinking. Originally, for the first issue, he supplied me with layouts, with the grids and stuff because he had a specific way, a very cinematic way of presenting the panel-to-panel work. Once I got a hold of that, we've come up with our own secret language where he'll just call me up and say, 'Change the so-and-so with blah-blah-blah' and I'll *know* what that means! And I'll change the so-and-so and blah-blah-blah so we're definitely on the same wavelength. His sense of visuals comes through very clearly."

The newest news in regards to *Powers* is the recently announced movie deal at Sony with Mace Neufeld, producers of "Men in Black." Oeming is excited by it all, but keeps calm about it, because no matter how cool a *Powers* movie could be "I haven't seen it yet," so he's withholding a certain level of enthusiasm. "What really happens when you make a deal -- and we have a really good deal, and when I say 'good deal' I mean we're well respected by the company. We're being treated very fairly, but the movie is out of our hands, so we just sit back and hope they make a good film. They have a good track record, Mace Neufeld are just widely know for doing quality stuff, so that's on our side."

But while the comic awaits Hollywood treatment, the book itself continues to work its magic on the public. In fact, in most outlets, issues can't be found. Oeming explains that "the reason we're going to trade paperback so quickly is because we basically sold out of the book. We *way* overprinted, but the reorders were so high, there's not enough to go around anymore!

In fact, something completely new will be coming out in the near future. As Oeming describes: "Brian and I do a lot of research for out projects and before I actually started *Powers* I went to the local police station and introduced myself. I got to do ride-alongs, I met the captain, I took extensive photo reference of all their equipment, they let me shoot a couple of rounds off at some criminals…wait, what was the original question? I got distracted and all excited about shooting people." he laughs.

Back on topic, Oeming tells the origin of what will be the *Powers Superhero Safety Coloring Book*. "So hanging around at the police station, you start noticing all the little knickknacks they have laying around. And one of those things is something for kids … safety coloring books! Big cartoony cops saying, 'Hey kids, if you see power lines down, don't touch them!' I sent Brain some as kind of a joke and he said, 'This is a great idea!' So the *Powers Coloring Book* will be a variation of this. You'll have safety tips like 'If you're walking down the street and you see two superhero beings fighting this guy and fire is blasting out of their eyes, immediately duck and cover.' 'Do not touch flame retardant superheroes…' It's safety tips for the *Powers* universe. Kind of like kids during the A-bomb scare, but there's superheroes flying out of the sky! We're going to be making some pretty good jokes about ourselves and the process of doing the book. It'll be fun."

A big jump from what they normally do, when you think about it. And Oeming laughs and

MORE GREAT BOOKS FROM IMAGE COMICS

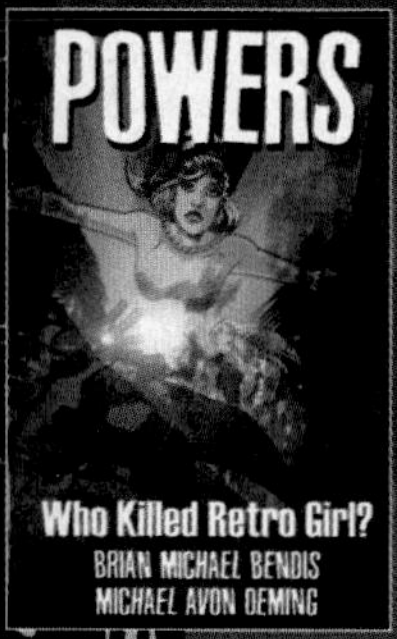
POWERS
Who Killed Retro Girl?
BRIAN MICHAEL BENDIS
MICHAEL AVON OEMING

POWERS, VOL. 1: WHO KILLED RETRO GIRL? TP
ISBN# 1-58240-669-3
$21.99

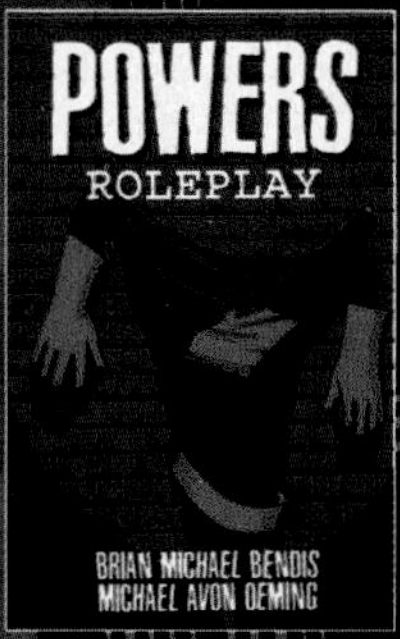
POWERS
ROLEPLAY
BRIAN MICHAEL BENDIS
MICHAEL AVON OEMING

POWERS, VOL. 2: ROLEPLAY TP
ISBN# 1-58240-695-2
$13.99

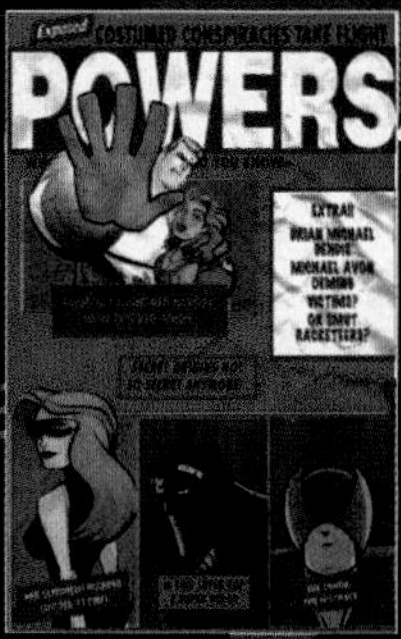
POWERS.

POWERS, VOL. 3: LITTLE DEATHS TP
ISBN# 1-58240-670-7
$19.99

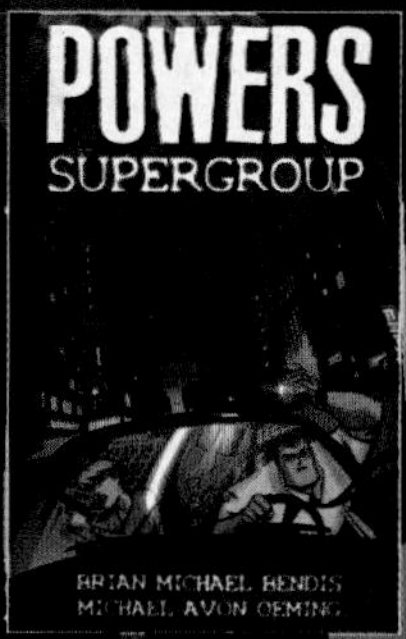
POWERS
SUPERGROUP
BRIAN MICHAEL BENDIS
MICHAEL AVON OEMING

POWERS, VOL. 4: SUPERGROUP TP
ISBN# 1-58240-671-5
$21.99

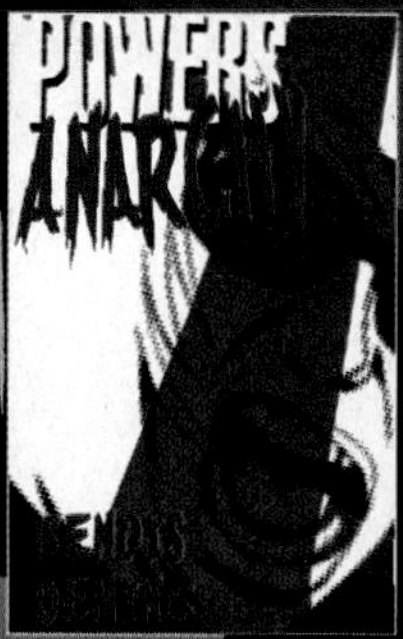

POWERS, VOL. 5: ANARCHY TP
ISBN# 1-58240-331-7
$14.95

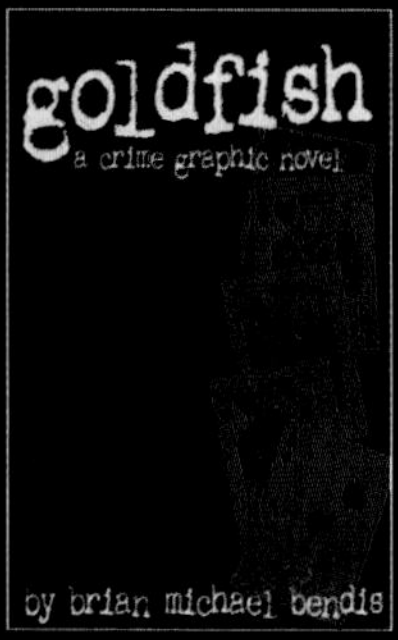
goldfish
a crime graphic novel
by brian michael bendis

GOLDFISH: THE DEFINITIVE COLLECTION TP
ISBN# 1-58240-195-0
$19.95

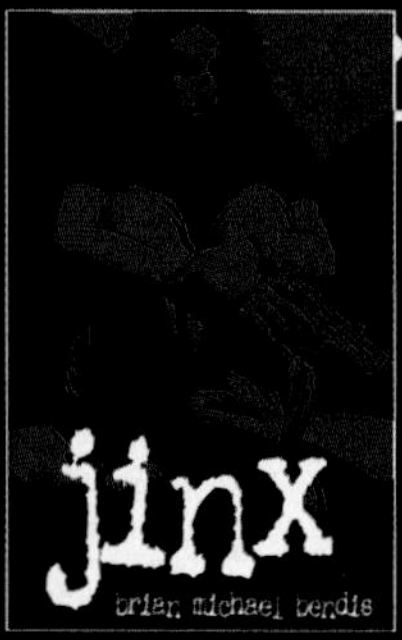
jinx
brian michael bendis

JINX: THE DEFINITIVE COLLECTION TP
ISBN# 1-58240-179-9
$24.95

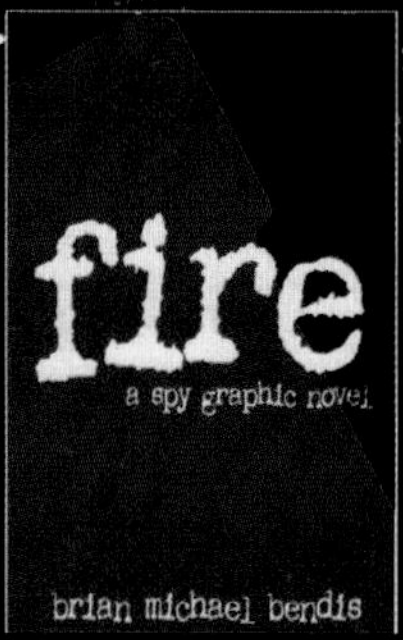
fire
a spy graphic novel
brian michael bendis

FIRE: THE DEFINITIVE COLLECTION TP
ISBN# 1-58240-071-7
$9.95

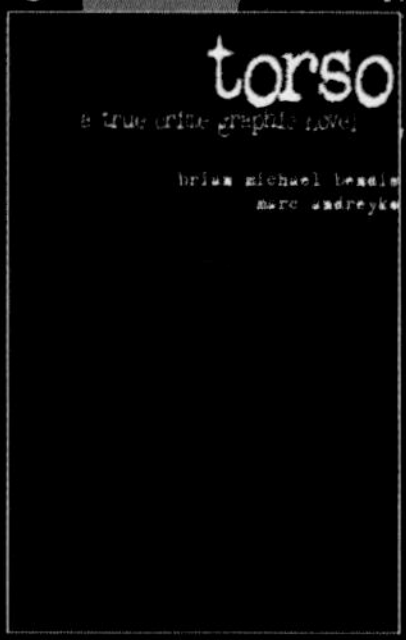
torso

TORSO: THE DEFINITIVE COLLECTION TP
ISBN# 1-58240-174-8
$21.95

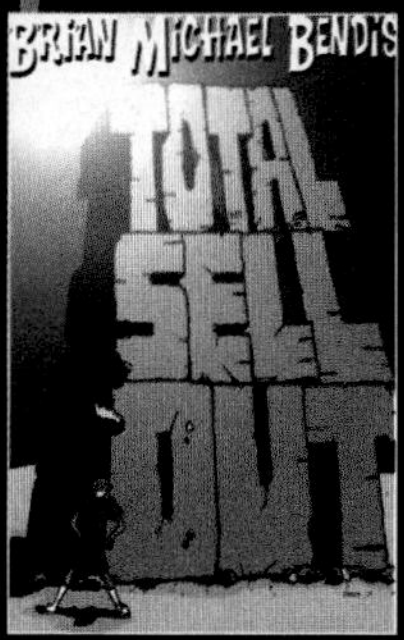
BRIAN MICHAEL BENDIS
TOTAL SELL OUT

TOTAL SELL OUT TP
ISBN# 1-58240-287-6
$14.95

ALSO AVAILABLE

40 OZ. COLLECTED TP
ISBN# 1-58240-329-5
$9.95

BAD IDEAS: COLLECTED! TP
ISBN# 1-58240-531-X
$12.99

CLASSIC 40 OZ.: TALES FROM THE BROWN BAG TP
ISBN# 1-58240-438-0
$14.95

DIORAMAS, A LOVE STORY GN
ISBN# 1-58240-359-7
$12.95

BLOOD RIVER GN
ISBN# 1-58240-509-3
$7.99

WINGS OF ANASI GN
$6.99

KABUKI

VOL. 1: CIRCLE OF BLOOD TP
ISBN# 1-88727-980-6
$19.95

VOL. 2: DREAMS TP
ISBN# 1-58240-277-9
$12.95

VOL. 3: MASKS OF NOH TP
ISBN# 1-58240-108-X
$12.95

VOL. 4: SKIN DEEP TP
ISBN# 1-58240-000-8
$12.95

VOL. 5: METAMORPHOSIS TP
ISBN# 1-58240-203-5
$24.99

VOL. 6: SCARAB TP
ISBN# 1-58240-258-2
$19.95

NIGHT TRIPPERS GN
ISBN# 1-58240-606-5
$16.99

NOWHERESVILLE TP
ISBN# 1-58240-241-8
$14.95

THE FURTHER ADVENTURES OF ONE PAGE FILLER MAN TP
ISBN# 1-58240-535-2
$11.99

GIRLS

VOL. 1: CONCEPTION TP
ISBN# 1-58240-529-8
$14.99

VOL. 2: EMERGENCE TP
ISBN# 1-58240-608-1
$14.99

GRRL SCOUTS

VOL. 1: TP
ISBN# 1-58240-316-3
$12.95

VOL. 2: WORK SUCKS TP
ISBN# 1-58240-343-0
$12.95

HAMMER OF THE GODS, VOL. 1: MORTAL ENEMY TP
ISBN# 1-58240-271-X
$18.95

POWERS SCRIPTBOOK
ISBN# 1-58240-233-7
$19.95

PUTTIN THE BACKBONE BACK TP
ISBN# 1-58240-402-X
$9.95

QUIXOTE NOVEL
ISBN# 1-58240-434-8
$9.95

SAN AND TWITCH: THE BRIAN MICHAEL BENDIS COLLECTION, VOL. 1 TP
ISBN# 1-58240-583-2
$24.95

SIX GN
ISBN# 1-58240-398-8
$5.95

STUPID COMICS, VOL. 1 TP
ISBN# 1-58240-611-1
$12.99

ULTRA: SEVEN DAYS TP
ISBN# 1-58240-483-6
$17.95

WHISKEY DICKEL, INTERNATIONAL COWGIRL GN
ISBN# 1-58240-318-X
$12.95

For a comic shop near you carrying graphic novels from Image Comics, please call toll free:
1-888-COMIC-BOOK